fulfilled

fulfilled

joey lankford

The Refreshing Alternative to the Half-Empty Life

PUBLISHING GROUP

NASHVILLE, TENNESSEE

978-1-4336-8153-0

Published by B&H Publishing Group
Nashville, Tennessee

Dewey Decimal Classification: 248.4
Subject Heading: GOD—WILL \ PROVIDENCE AND
GOVERNMENT OF GOD \ CHRISTIAN LIFE

1 2 3 4 5 6 7 8 9 • 19 18 17 16 15 14

This book is dedicated to the one who
has prayed for me, encouraged me, loved me,
and at times, pulled me along on this journey of faith.
I love you, Courtney Lankford.

Contents

Foreword

I regularly meet people who feel empty. They're good Christians. They love Jesus. They may be active at church, volunteering in their community, and supporting local and overseas ministries. They're doing all the Christian stuff, but still a sense of emptiness nags at them. There is a feeling that the Christian life should be greater, more significant. It shouldn't leave you asking yourself: *Is this all?*

The adventure that God invites each of us on is a life filled with meaning and purpose. His plan for each of us is unique, but it is always filled with a sense of passion to complete God's mission to demonstrate and share His love. He may send you to Wall Street or the local soup kitchen. He may ask you to spend years in preparation or to drop everything and start doing what you feel totally unprepared to do. But just as God called my friend Joey Lankford on an exciting adventure that he could never have previously imagined, He is also calling you.

Joey Lankford had it all, a great and exciting job, a wonderful family, and all the toys a thirty-five-year-old could dream of. On the surface, it must have seemed perfect, but apparently you didn't need to dig too deep to see that something was wrong. Joey later told me that a woman at his office put a copy of my first book, *The Hole in Our Gospel*, in front of his door. The book recounts my own discovery of how God called me to a more significant Christian life. Apparently the secret was out on Joey's "half-empty life."

That's how it was for me. I remember considering the offer to become president of World Vision, and I was torn up inside. I was terrified of what my life would become if I wholeheartedly said *yes* to God's call. Today, I cringe at the thought that I almost said no. I have found greater joy and passion doing what God asked of me than doing anything else I've ever done. I'm discovering new talents, meeting amazing people, seeing extraordinary things, and I get to live and work on the front lines of God's movement around the world. What a privilege.

We only get to experience that joy, however, when we have done what God asks of us. The Christian life is more than simply going to church and checking off the right list of items in order to get to heaven when we die.

When we sign our life to Christ, it is like enlisting in the military. We go where we are assigned to go, and we do the tasks our commanding officer asks. Retiring in Boca Raton or spending weekends in Vegas is out of the question. We are in training for a mission. God asks us to lay everything down at His feet—our reputation, our money, our status. He may allow us to keep all those things and use us right where we are, but He may also ask us to give it all up in order to give us something better. He wants us to give that choice to Him.

That's what Joey discovered. He had enlisted, you might say, but was living a civilian life until his draft number came up. What Joey found—and what so many others who tell me their stories also discover—is that they wouldn't trade the amazing adventure of being on God's mission for an ordinary life pursuing the American Dream. People questioned Joey, his reputation suffered, and even other Christians doubted what God had called him to do. Yet he also saw tantalizing hints that God was calling him elsewhere. Hints from his family, his business, and his church. God was making it clear He had a mission for Joey, but in order to embrace it he had to let go of everything else.

Joey now gets to use his God-given abilities to do what God cares most about—demonstrating His love to a broken world, restoring, redeeming, and reclaiming this world for Christ. Living in South Africa, Joey is able to work on behalf of people in poverty, helping them discover an abundant life in Jesus Christ. In a racially torn country, Joey's own family is a witness for Jesus' love for all people. Joey lives out the gospel for people who would never have given an ear to a preacher, but who see in Joey and his family's daily life a way to understand the saving message of Jesus Christ.

I don't know what God might be calling you to do. It might be to serve Him right where you are, or it might be a call to forsake everything and follow Him somewhere else, somewhere out of your comfort zone. Either way, God simply asks that you be willing and available—no strings attached.

So when you have finished this book and feel inspired by Joey's life, as you surely will, be prepared to take a leap of faith toward God's plan for your life. And don't look back.

Richard Stearns
President, World Vision U.S.
Bellevue, Washington

Introduction

Satisfied?

just remember it being really bright. A big field. Front porch. Beautiful day. Wildflowers. Birds singing. Lots of sun, lots of color. It was quiet—country quiet—the kind of quiet where the wind carries your grandkids' voices all the way up from down the hill where they're playing. Splashing in the creek, getting dirty, squealing when one of the little boys picks up a grasshopper or crawdad and tries to put it in his sister's hair.

I laughed to myself when I saw it, sitting there. Remembering when one of those crazy, barefoot, trouble-making boys was me.

But look at me now. King of my castle. The Lankford family farm. My shirt open a couple of buttons, my skinny old man legs poking out all white and hairless underneath a pair of blue jean shorts, a cold drink in my hand, and a nice breeze cooling the beads of sweat on my chest and forehead. I was homegrown success, rocking back on a full career of making friends and brokering deals, enjoying the kind of Saturday afternoon where your money's finally working for *you* instead of you working so hard for your money.

Felt good.

Felt . . . perfect.

I even thought I heard my wife kicking around in the kitchen, talking and laughing with the others in there, maybe putting together some stuff for me to throw on the grill here in a little while. If I leaned back far enough, I could almost see her through the window right behind me.

But wait—*that* didn't look like my wife in there. And wait—I don't remember ever being this old. And I don't have any grandkids! I've just got my *three* kids, and the oldest one's barely school-age yet.

Who are all these people around here? And who am I? Where *are* we?

Then all of a sudden, I realized. God was painting a picture for me. A picture *of* me. If He were to draw a straight line through my life, trace it all the way up till now, then poke it through and run that string all the way out to my sixty-fifth birthday—this was where it was taking me. Right here. On this front porch. With maybe my wife inside or maybe another one. With maybe all my kids and grandkids here or maybe just the ones who'll still speak to me. With maybe a heart that's full and content

2

or maybe one that's just full of ambition, never satisfied, always reaching for more, more, more, always more.

I don't know. I couldn't tell. I just know the longer I looked, the emptier I felt. Was this it? Is this what I was working seventy hours a week for? Is this all you get at the end—a bunch of maybes? A few nice Saturday afternoons a year? A nice place to live but an all-consuming life, the kind that forever has its hand out and its mouth open, constantly demanding to be fed and watered and updated and insured? Everything you need but nothing you want?

And what if I'd been supposed to do something else? What if God had given me a choice back when I was, say, thirty years old: I could come *here* or I could go with *Him*? Where *He's* going? Where *He* could take me? To watch what *He* could do with my family? To see what *He* could create from my work and my business? To discover what *He* would paint for my future if I put the brush entirely in His hand and spread out my arms like a wide-open canvas and said . . . *Go for it! Do it!* Whatever You say. Do it now. Just don't leave me old and empty!

I didn't want to go there.

I *still* don't want to go there.

God, please, don't make me go there.

And if you feel the same way, if you share the same dread of ending up empty when it's all said and done, when it's too late to do any different, when you're too old to care anymore, I sure am glad you found your way to this book—because we've got some things in common.

I've decided I'm not dying empty. I'm not cashing in all my work at retirement age and being paid back in nothing but regrets. I'm not selling out just so I can hold on to what I've got. Not playing it safe. Not letting somebody else tell me what success is supposed to look like and dress like and count up to. Not expecting my 401k to determine how wisely I've invested my life. Not rolling up in a truck that cost me fifteen thousand extra dollars just to be sure I'd impress you with it.

I don't want it. Do you?

If you're a dyed-in-the-wool American Dreamer, there's probably not a lot I can do for you. In fact, if you happened to keep your receipt, I'm sure you can probably get your money back at the bookstore or see if they'll trade you for a couple of magazines or a beach novel. Sounds like you've got better stuff to do than to read this.

Been nice talking to you.

But if you're still here, if you're like me, if you've seen what you get, even after you've busted it hard, checking off all the right boxes and following all the directions, then let's stick this out a little longer, okay? I'm not much of a writer, and maybe you're not much of a reader, but I think between the two of us, God might do something really special. A lot more special than some high-priced, hyper-inflated, hollowed-out American Dream.

He's sure doing it for me. And for my family.

Not because we deserve it or because we're anything special. Not because I'm so smart and superior, like I've figured everything out. Bottom line, I just got really tired of my life being an accumulation contest. Constantly tripping over the toys. (Theirs and mine.) I got tired of the stress and pressure, both from within myself and from nonstop life in general—not because I was too good to be bothered by the same things everybody else deals with, but because pushing against it just never seemed to be getting me anywhere. No matter what I did, I just kept working my way back to the same old place, the same old questions, the same old junk, the same old stumbling blocks, the same old issues, different only by the details and the decade. I got tired of being disappointed, knowing I needed to change but never being *able* to change. Not for long. Not as soon as things smoothed out again. Then I'd just go back to being who I am . . . even if that's the same person who always ends up making me want to be somebody different. Every stinkin' time.

As a believer in Christ, I got sick of reading the Bible and going to church and getting nothing out of it but the conviction part, the help-us-in-the-nursery part, the go-on-another-men's-retreat part. And even when it seemed like this was what I was supposed to be doing as a husband and father, when God really did seem big and amazing to me in those worshipful moments, something still just felt so empty about it most of the time. I mean, the Bible says He could part the Red Sea and turn water into wine. He could raise a man back from the dead. And yet Christian life *to me* was like—you know, like, complaining to Him when I was running late and the traffic was backed up. Stuff like that.

Obviously something wasn't right.

He was up *there*, and I was down *here*. And I just wasn't connecting the two. People *thought* I was getting it, because I was loud and bold and jumping around and God seemed to be blessing me. But whenever I'd be alone or would quiet down long enough to see what was really going on, I could tell—something was disjointed here.

Was I happy? Mmm . . . I guess. Yeah.

But satisfied? Fired up? Fulfilled?

No way. Unh-uh.

And I think you know exactly what I'm talking about.

I don't have all the answers for you. A lot of that can only be worked out between you and God, between you and your family, between you and yourself. But I can tell you this: You don't have to be empty. You weren't *made* to be empty. And if God can get that big idea through to a head as hard and leathery as mine, I know He can get through to you.

There's a fuller life out there for you. It'll cost you some things you probably don't want to pay, things you may not think you can risk. I ain't lying to you, it'll mess with your plans for the weekend. But every one of us, every day that we tie our futures to our own plans, our own expectations, our own guidelines, our own terms— it may not feel like it, but we're risking. Risking an old guy on his front porch, discovering far too late where American Dreams go to die.

Chapter 1

Call Me Crazy

We were somewhere along I-40 in East Tennessee when the call came in, middle of the day, driving home from a weekend trip to my little brother's wedding. I didn't recognize the number when it popped up on my phone display. All I could tell was that it didn't originate from anywhere around here. Weird-looking number. Should I take it? *Yeah, take it.*

I took it.

And no wonder the number looked funny. It was Jacques, our landlord, calling from France, the guy who owned our rental house in Kommetjie (don't try to sound it out; it's COM-uh-key)—a suburb of Cape Town, out along the western coast of South Africa.

"What's up?" I asked him.

"Joey, I need to tell you something. I've gotten a cash offer on the house. An international buyer is willing to give me my asking price." He was talking about the house we lived in, the house where all our stuff was currently located while we were home in the States on furlough— the house we'd been led to believe we could occupy for as long as we wanted to stay there. "And I'm trying to figure out what to do," he said.

"Well . . ." I thought, realizing it wasn't exactly my call to make, "I guess you ought to sell it. You've got a cash offer. There aren't a lot of buyers coming along, not in this economy, so . . . I understand. I'm a businessman. If it was me, that's what I'd do. Sounds like an offer you can't refuse." I knew he hadn't gotten so much as a nibble from six months of trying to sell it previously. And the last I'd heard, he was letting the contract with his realtor expire.

"Yes, I know, Joey, but . . ."

Oh. There was more.

". . . they want you out immediately."

Okay, that *does* make it different. The 298-mile marker we were sailing past on the interstate at that particular moment was more than *eight thousand* miles away from the house he was referring to. So we were obviously in no position to begin moving our belongings out of it—and *wouldn't* be for at least another couple of weeks. Maybe more. Maybe a *lot* more, depending on how quickly we could find another place to stay. All I knew was, when we signed up on mission, when we sold every- thing and moved our whole family to South Africa on the subtext of following God's will, this out-of-the-blue, out-immediately plan wasn't the one we'd bargained for.

Think fast, Joey.

"I don't know what to tell you, Jacques. I mean, I'm in America right now, so I can't really do anything about it. If that's the way it needs to be, I guess they can buy all my furniture, and my Land Rover, and do something with Rimshot, my dog."

"I know, Joey," he said, apologetically. "I understand it's a real problem, I do. And of course, by contract, I don't even need to ask you. I can just go ahead and finalize the sale, but"—this is the part that floored me, changed the whole way I was feeling—"Nellie and I have been following you and your family, reading about you on your website, and I must say, you people have truly crept into our hearts. That's why we're having such a hard time making a decision about this—especially on these terms."

I don't know what shocked me more—a nowhere-near Christian couple in Europe that I should never have met in my lifetime sensing the love of God through a redneck country boy like me, or the words my wife was about to speak a few minutes later when I finally hung up the phone.

I had done the best I could do to buy us some time. Jacques said he'd try to get us ninety days before we'd need to vacate and find new arrangements. But when I glanced over and gave that look to Courtney—the one person in our family who's the epitome of planning and control, of calendars and organization, the one most likely to *freak* at the way this unexpected change was sure to unsettle us—she instead let out a short little sigh, which curled into one of her cute little smiles, and said, "Well, I guess since God has allowed this to happen . . . can you imagine the blessing He's got waiting for us?"

Ordinarily, just being honest with you: No. *But when you put it that way, Court*—

Then yes.

Yes, I can.

Because, hey, I was looking at His blessing already! My wife and I would *never* have been unflappable enough to take this kind of news lying down, not even while I was back making six figures every year and could more easily afford the distraction. Back when we didn't think twice about putting our next unnecessary purchase on a credit card. Back when spending $500 apiece on our kids' presents at Christmas was nothing. Back when the next big decision on our plate was whether or not to build out our basement, and how big to do it.

But now—right then—rolling down the highway, apparently and suddenly homeless, with our four kids in the back (one of them a little girl we'd recently adopted from Ethiopia), our immediate, gut response was a grin and a laugh and a, "Well, here goes! Can't wait to see where He takes us from *here.*"

I know. It's crazy. Isn't it? And I swear, if the old Joey—the one who'd been peeping out of these same eyeballs the first thirty years of my life—could've somehow leaned his head in between us in the front seat, looked quizzically at me, then at Courtney, then back at me again, he'd have said, "You guys are nuts!" And maybe we were. Maybe we are.

But for me, I'll take this crazy life over anybody else's. I'll even take it over the one I'd been trying to orchestrate all on my own before—because this one, this life God has chosen to lead us on, is making us about ten thousand times happier than we've ever been in our lives. I've never loved my wife as much as I love her now (and I'm pretty sure she'd say the same about me . . . on most days, I think). Our kids have never had less, and yet I can promise you they've never been more achieving and content. Our life is so full of adventure and meaning and everyday purpose—of people and relationships and opportunities for ministry—I really don't even know how to start writing about it.

I just know it's real. I just know it can happen. I just know it fires me up.

I've seen it on I-40.

And now I see it twenty-four hours a day.

Calling All Trailblazers

God called me away from a lucrative job, complete with stock options and a secure future, with a 4,500-square-foot house on seven acres in the most beautiful spot on earth (or so I thought). And yet today, by His grace and perhaps ironic sense of humor after leading us to walk away from it all, I wake up every morning with the breeze of the Atlantic Ocean misting through the open windows

in our bedroom, with whales often pounding their huge
bodies in the distant surf, with the rise of towering mountains clearly visible behind me. And sometimes when I
look out on the mind-blowing geography here on this
amazingly colorful tip of the African continent, I can
almost hear God saying, "You know how for thirty years
you tried to box Me in, Joey? You know how you limited
what you thought I could do? Well, check this out, son."

Some sacrifice.

No, we're not living in the lap of luxury. We're not
vacationing here. We do without a lot of things we once
enjoyed, most important, the people we used to enjoy
them with. My car only runs about three days a week, and
there's no college football on television Saturday afternoons. We have no air, no heat, a tiny refrigerator that
only holds enough food for a couple of days, and baboons
that break into our house three or four times a year—real
ones—rummaging through our cabinets, slinging stuff all
over the place, stealing everything down to our chewing
gum.

But for the first time in my life, I've got everything.
Not a problem-free existence, and not a perfect display of
Christian lifestyle, but the complete, absolute confidence
of being dead-on in the will of God and a hundred percent sure He's taking care of me and my family. No doubt.
Serving Him isn't something I feel forced to try tacking on
at the end of the week anymore, like I'm doing Him some
big favor. Watching Him work and knowing He's real isn't
something that takes a lot of effort for us now. It's just

what we do. It's how we live. We need Him. We can't get by without Him.

Why did we think we were better off not knowing that? Not doing that?

My life before launching out on this new journey with God looked pretty perfect from the outside. There were times of day, in fact, when it even felt perfect on the inside. But in reality—tell me if you can't relate to this—my "perfect" life was a lot like the dog trails that ran around the side of our house in College Grove, Tennessee, going *somewhere* but mainly going *nowhere*.

Everybody who owns an outdoor dog has a dog trail in the yard. Dogs go the same way every time. They get up, then they go over there. Do that, then come back over here. They beat the same path to the same bowl to the same dry dog food every day, and that's just what they do. And they don't care. Because they're dogs.

But how is that pattern of life so much different from the one I'd been running? Get up, go to work, do my thing, bust my can, make it to Friday night, see who's coming over, get up on Saturday, cut the grass, piddle around, go to a birthday party or something, come in late, maybe get to church in time for Sunday school the next morning, maybe not, hit the worship service at least, go out to eat together afterwards—and that's the drill. Everybody does it. And everybody wonders why it keeps circling back to the same old bowl every time.

Because that's what ruts do. They always lead you back to the same place. I see it even in Africa, people walking every day on those beaten-down trails. Eyes fixed. Single file. Not stepping off to the right or the left, just going ahead, then coming back. Same thing tomorrow. Same thing the next day.

That road. That rut. The same Ol' Roy in the same old bowl.

Yeah, we can pretty it up all we want. Put it in a high-rise office building. Drive it to work in a $50,000 car. Feed it a nice lunch. Give it a sharp business card. Grow it into a good, healthy return and a fine personal reputation. Sit it down in church on Sunday and shake everybody's hand with it on your way out.

But it's still a rut.

And it still doesn't satisfy.

It's empty. And keeps getting emptier.

For a long time in my life, I'd been developing routines that weren't taking me anywhere. Only in circles. Oh, sometimes I'd come around the corner with a new toy or a new piece of gear in hand—a new bone to chew on for a day or two. But eventually I recognized that no matter how much junk I dragged home at the end of the day, the week, the month, I was never getting off this thing—this rut—not unless I did something drastic, something radical, not unless I somehow found a way to jump this comfortable little dog trail that felt so normal and offered so little.

I'm not knocking hard work, obviously. I work as hard now as I ever did. Harder. Nor am I trying to minimize faithful, consistent effort or to act like being steady and responsible is a problem to be avoided, like it's almost wrong to be so loyal and dependable. No, I'm just asking you the same kind of questions I ultimately asked myself: What's the goal here? Where are you going? And when you get there—five years from now, twenty years from now, forty years from now—is it going to be worth it?

Will you look back and say, "What—was I *crazy*? To think this was going to do it for me?"

One November recently, eight young to middle-age businessmen—CEOs, some of them—came over to South Africa for a weeklong visit. "How did you do it?" they wanted to know. "How did you make this move?" I could see it in their eyes, just like I've seen it in others, just like I've seen it in my own. They want to be free. Not from responsibility, but from the rut. They want their faith to be relevant somehow, not just a relish tray, not just a little something extra for them on the side. They want to know they're putting their eggs in the right basket. And if so, they're all-in.

I've given my testimony numerous times at churches and other places back home. Men invariably come up to me afterward, "Can we meet sometime, Joey? I want to hear more about what you're doing. I really felt something come alive inside while you were speaking, something that's been stirring in me for a long time." They sense the gap between where they are and where they want to be. They want the abundant life they haven't been able to locate in the places they've been looking for it. Nothing's really wrong with them or with their lives. And yet *everything's* wrong. Their wives know something's wrong. Their kids suspect something's wrong. Most of all, *they* know something's wrong. They're slapping shoe leather every day, and yet their gauge is slapping empty when they're finished. Almost every time.

They're not faithless. They're not trying to run from porn addictions or looking to get out of their marriages. They're not bad people without a clue of what they're doing. They just want to feel alive again. Their hearts want to embrace a calling rather than just a career. They want the rush of being out there where trusting God is raw and real and ripe with opportunity.

Most of them have so much stuff around them, they don't even *need* God. From the look of things, they've got their lives kind of covered. Or at least it feels like it. And honestly, there's a big part of them that wishes they could just go along like this, without being bothered by His little guilt trips, without feeling pulled in His direction, away from what they want and when they want it.

But in their gut, they know. They *do* need Him. They *must* have Him! Their insides are crying out for Him. There's got to be more. More than this. More than what they're seeing. More than where this is all going.

Yes, there is.

And I don't care who you are or where you're from. I don't care how much trouble you've given God in the past or how much time you've wasted and frittered away leading up to this point. Your life can start taking a turn in the direction of fulfillment this afternoon or by tonight.

Don't plan on quitting your job in the morning or anything, but I'll tell you what—you can sure begin making pullout plans from your little rut by then. You do not have to stay there. Even if you don't change where you live or where you work, you can pivot yourself in a new direction that'll begin steering you toward a much more satisfying place and lifestyle than your dog trails ever can.

And if you think this freed-up person couldn't possibly be you . . .

If you're skeptical about how the difference it might make could possibly offset the lack of security and control it would entail . . .

If you don't know how you'd explain yourself to people who notice you're not acting the way you always did before . . .

If your mind is racing already, lobbing up excuses, telling you to settle down, keep your composure, don't get carried away with this guy's craziness . . . then, man, you don't know what God is able to do. Because if He can create a turnaround in somebody like me, if He can do what He's done to break this maverick spirit and harness it for something that even vaguely resembles His glory, I guarantee you He can do it in anybody.

And I do mean *anybody.*

How Crazy Do You Think I Am?

When my parents pulled up stakes during my ninth-grade year to move our family into the next county over, into a whole different neighborhood and environment, one reason they did it was because of me. Not to get me into a better school district, but to keep me out of trouble. Hopefully.

It mostly didn't work.

I'm the oldest of five—two boys on each end, one girl in the middle. And I was able to prove to everybody that reckless behavior doesn't typically recognize the county line. Oh, I wasn't doing anything really bad, just a lot of mischievousness and rank immaturity. Always trying to be the life of the party, the cutup, the cheap entertainment, even if it meant being a real jerk to do it.

Funny, I was a Christian through it all. Saved when I was eight. Baptized by my grandfather. (I've still got the picture in my Bible to prove it.) My own parents, too, were the living model for how you do that job right— steady, loving, godly, aware, firm, patient, consistent. I didn't have anybody to blame except myself if I was bent on misbehaving.

But like a lot of people, I got good at playing both sides of the religion game. I could be the good little church boy when the situation called for it, and I could be the renegade hellion when nobody else was the wiser. And by the time I'd met the girl that I'd decided I wanted to marry, I followed her all the way to a small Christian college in Texas—not to study, not to quit my antics, but just to get engaged.

And we did. It was great. For a while. But not being too motivated to hit the books, I did a lot more hitting the town instead. And as my girlfriend started to look at me through the eyes of marriage material rather than just the misty glow of teenage hormones, she decided—understandably, level-headedly—she might be about to make a big mistake. With me.

Level heads might have prevailed, I'm sure, but mine just went into free fall. As soon as she broke our relationship off—engagement and everything—I went wilder than ever. I was already thirteen hours away from home, clear of everybody's radar screen, and I decided at that time I'd just make the most of a paid-up tuition and live it up for the rest of the semester. I'd party like a madman, fail every class, and then finally go home to tell my dad I needed to start over someplace else. That's just the way I was thinking back then.

Those two years of college (if you can call it that) were all I ever completed. No diploma at the end. And no real desire for one. The only thing I really had going for me when I got back to Tennessee was my dad's offer to drive a truck for his medical supply company, taking hospital beds and oxygen tanks and wheelchairs and stuff out to people's homes, setting them up, breaking them down. It was blue-color work at hourly pay, but it was better than nothing. My parents sure weren't putting me back in school right away, not with my four other siblings following right up behind me.

But oddly enough, I found myself getting interested in how my father's business worked. I'd been raised around it, of course, and I was distantly familiar with it, but I'd never really thought much about the whole process. Running a company. Managing a budget. Evaluating growth strategies. Negotiating purchasing agreements with vendors. Now that I was hanging around as an employee, I found this corporate aspect to be kind of exciting. Challenging. I wanted more of it. And I hoped my dad would give me a chance to grow into it.

So after a few years—after proving I could keep myself steady, after being given some step-up promotions with gradually increasing responsibilities—I eventually became the guy who managed all the day-to-day operations, overseeing eighty-five employees and professionals providing contract services, as well as a $100,000 payroll every two weeks. Running the show. Life was good.

Life with Courtney made it even better. We had met (actually gotten reacquainted) after I came back from college, then married in April 2000, and the kids started coming soon thereafter—Briley, Braxton, and Barron—filling out our home with all the required elements for the American Dream. Beautiful wife. Beautiful children. Beautiful piece of property in the country, away from the city lights but not inconveniently far away from good shopping, good restaurants, and lots of fun things to do. I had the horse barn. The man cave. The hunting gear. The new vehicles. The rollicking four-wheeler.

We were set up. Supposedly for life. Secure. Solid family. Everybody on both sides—parents, siblings, in-laws, cousins—all within little more than a fifteen-mile radius, the promise of anytime babysitting and all-the-time support and connectedness.

Let's just put it this way: none of this story of mine adds up to missions work. For starters, who'd be crazy enough to see potential in me? No college degree. No theological training. A lot more stupidity than spiritual growth in my track record.

And on top of that, what thirty-year-old would be crazy enough to bail from what appeared to be the beginnings of big-time success? Early wealth and accomplishment. A comfortable, affluent lifestyle. Loving, caring, well-heeled people and friends all around me.

You're right. It'd be crazy.

Unless you mean crazy good.

Fill 'Er Up

If God hadn't done what He did for me, if He hadn't finally given me the sense to realize He was right—about everything—I don't know where I'd be today.

Just guessing, I'd say I'd still be making good money, cutting new deals, always trying to one-up the competition, driving an even newer truck than the one I'd been driving before. I'd be reaching certain goals and benchmarks I'd set for myself, and I wouldn't be letting anything stop me from getting anything I wanted at Bass Pro Shop. People would wish they could be like Joey Lankford, to have what he has.

But not if they really knew. Because nothing else in my life would've been growing at the same speed as my wallet. My spiritual life wouldn't be progressing. Hardly at all. I wouldn't be any more loving or content or trusting or prayerful, except in emergencies. I wouldn't know what it meant to be happy. Not really. I wouldn't be ready for trouble when it came. I'd carry inside myself the illusion—and would present it this way to others—that I was big and strong and untouchable and resilient. But I'd crumble if life got too hard. I know I would. I'd run. I'd bolt. My threshold for what I'd tolerate in riding out difficulties would be pretty low.

My idea of life with God, on a daily, practical level, would be whatever I thought He could do for me. Sure, I'd put some sizable checks in the collection plate on occasion. I'd score some noticeable points on the Joe Christian scale. But I wouldn't know what God was really capable of. And so I wouldn't know all the things He was capable of accomplishing, not just *for* me, but *in* me and *through* me.

I'd be full, yes—like *stuffed* full after a big, heavy meal. Belt open. Belching. Groggy from gorging myself.

And I'd be empty at the same time.

Because I'd know I'd just get hungry again.

That's really all we can expect from the average American life—even the good life. And yet somehow, thanks in large part to the Deceiver of our souls, we're fool enough to think it'll somehow prove different for us. That new house with the extra space really will make up for what we've been lacking. That new customer or client, if we can land him, will finally put us where we always wanted to be in business. That new baby will settle us down. That new job will change everything.

No it won't.

It *can't*.

We'll burn through it all, we'll run it at high speeds, we'll put everything we've got into it, and—mark my words—we'll be toast at the end. Worse than the way we felt when we started. Burned out. Disappointed. Still screaming for something to be more and better than what this always turns out to be.

We're just crazy that way.

I don't know if that's where you are or not. I'm pretty sure that's where I'd be. Because that's where I was headed.

But there's hope for us, y'all. There's a fuller life out there. One that's full of God. Full of faith. Full of leaps and bounds in your growth and character. Full of peace. Full of passion.

A life full of transformation. Full of deep, authentic friendships. Full of vibrant excitement on a daily basis. Full of new marital strength and intimacy and a new level of relationship with your kids.

A life full of feel-good, give-it-away generosity. Full of a good day's work. Full of God's miraculous, on-time provision. Full of everything you've always wanted, full of everything you feel is missing when you look up and realize you've been tricked into thinking you had enough.

Abundant life is not just a Bible verse.

It's supposed to be a modern-day reality for God's people.

I don't know everything about it yet. But I know I've never experienced it like I'm experiencing it today.

Now listen, I still struggle with some of the same issues, habits, and bad attitudes that cropped up on me at the farm. Courtney and I still don't get it right a lot of times. Sometimes *all* the time, seems like. We still get frustrated with ourselves and with the obstacles of life as they come along. We're still very much on a journey, and we're not expecting to land at a destination anytime soon. We're a long, long way from perfect. We're living proof that God uses damaged, fallen people to accomplish His everyday wonders.

The difference now is that the big break we were always looking for—the one we always thought would settle and satisfy us—has come simply (and only) from being broken before the Lord. Just completely splayed out, flat on the ground, holding on together to keep from being blown away by the new challenges we face.

But what blows us away instead is where He's taking us in our relationship with Him, where He's taking our family, where He's taking our marriage, where He's taking the other people He allows us to touch and help and teach and listen to.

We thought we were so full.

But we had no idea what full was.

No, we're still not the people we want to be. Life's still hard. It still asks a lot of us. And it still leaves us with a lot of questions.

But we're sure not in a rut anymore. We're not empty. And it's not because of South Africa. It's because of something else. Something that's right where *you* live too, wherever you are—ready to be awakened, to put you on a whole new path, to take you to fullness.

There's only one thing to do.

Surrender . . .

Chapter 2

Writing on the Wall

M ike Glenn, pastor of our home church back in America, once said something I've never forgotten: "There will come a time in your life when you're going to need to be prepared. And you're not going to have time to *get* prepared."

For me, that time came on an ordinary weekday in April 2004, sitting through a morning business meeting at the office.

My cell phone had buzzed a few times in my pocket, and not wanting to be interrupted, I had deliberately chosen to ignore it. Finally, sensing I was stuck on somebody's redial, I fished it out to see who it was.

It was my wife. I guess that changes things.

"I'm on my way to the hospital, Joe. They think something's wrong."

Her water had apparently broken—maybe—at twenty-six and a half weeks, pregnant with our second child. When she hadn't been able to reach me, she'd called the doctor, who told her to meet him at the emergency room.

"Okay," I said, "you'll be all right," trying to calm the panic in her voice. "Call me back when you find out what's going on, and I'll get over there as quick as I can."

Hanging up, I returned my rattled attention to the papers and agenda points scattered around me on the conference table. That's when my eye caught the silent, head-shaking disbelief of eighty-year-old Charlie Green, my mentor and business friend, staring right at me. "Joey, son—if your wife is at the hospital, and you're still more worried about what we're going to say at the bank here at 11:30, you are way off track, hoss. *Get* out of here, and *get* over there!"

Right. Of course. You're right.

So it wasn't long before I was standing in a white room, listening to a white coat, who was telling me in his rough, thick, annoying German accent, "It appears, Mr. Lankford, your vife's contractions are happening too frequently for us to stop them. And so I just vahnt to prepare you. If we're able to get your baby here safely today, and if we can keep him alive, there's a good chance he von't be able to tie his shoes by the time he's ready for kindergarten."

Or something like that.

I swear, I don't know what kept me from hauling off and punching that guy square in the mouth right then. Dude was making me so angry.

He finally walked out—before I *threw* him out—and there I stood, all by myself, unable to go in to see Courtney at the moment because of the seriousness of her condition, just left alone to deal with the dawning realization that my life—our life—was suddenly, surprisingly, and very unexpectedly spinning completely out of my control.

And I was not prepared for it.

Have you ever been there? When getting mad won't fix it? When you can't work hard enough or long enough to fight through it or change it or overcome it? When you're either ready or you're not? When there's nobody you can call to come help pay what you owe, or tell you what to do, or make it all right for you in the end?

It's just you and God. And life and death.

And for the first time in a long time—if He's ever had it before—He's sure got your attention now.

Perhaps like you (if you can think back and put yourself in a similar moment), my life had pretty much been perfect up to that point. No serious sicknesses in my family. No broken marriages or strained relationships. Everybody who had died so far—even distant relatives—had all passed away at a ripe old age. We Lankfords, it seemed, just didn't have to put up with the kind of stuff I was facing right then. Or at least that's what I'd mistakenly led myself to believe.

Courtney and I—we were just about ready to have it all. We had the house, the dog, the career, the connections, all the plans in place for being financially independent by the age of thirty-five or forty, and only about three months away from having the two kids to match. The perfect set. But in the blink of an eye on a nice, normal, very routine spring morning—before my breakfast had even had time to digest—I was now looking at the real possibility of a handicapped child who (to hear Dr. von Doomsday tell it) wouldn't know his ABCs from his BVDs. Or worse, he might not even live long enough to take a single breath. He might, in fact, be dead already, for all I knew.

And Courtney—what was happening with Courtney? Was she going to be all right? I wasn't going to lose her *too*, was I?

My mom calls these situations "ironing board moments"—when you're pressed hard and pinned down, when life is suddenly all hard metal and steam, when you discover in real time and living color whether you're going to let God shape you into something He can actually wear, or you're going to keep thinking you'll be all right with all these wrinkles.

I don't mind admitting—especially now that Braxton's here, totally healthy, the most incredible little guy in the world—God exposed me that morning for who I was. And He proved to me that I wasn't ready. Wasn't ready to keep from being resistant to the fact that I wasn't in majority control of things . . . that *He* was . . . that He was in *complete* control. Not me.

But really, that wasn't the worst of it. Here's how stupid I was. Here's how stupid too many of us are. Because after seven whole weeks of my wife being in an eighth-floor hospital room, pumped full of magnesium to get her labor to regulate; after seven whole weeks of me sitting up nights with my little girl, Briley, wondering when her Mommy was ever coming home; after two more weeks in the NICU with Braxton, followed by another serious scare that put him back in the hospital for *another* emergency stay, it still wasn't long thereafter—once everything finally settled down to normal—that I went back to thinking I could manage just fine on my own from there.

I got it now, God, thanks.

You can go bail out somebody else now.

What's the matter with us? What gives us the fool notion that we're in charge of this thing? What turns us into these independent thinkers who decide we know what's best for us, even after we've been shown—in no uncertain terms—how seriously inadequate we are to handle certain situations? What makes us go so quickly and forgetfully from a low point like that to the place where we believe we don't really need His oversight and direction anymore? Sure, we'll keep Him on our advisory team, calling Him up if there's a crisis. Glad to know He's there for that. But otherwise we walk on. Unchanged.

*Sleep*walking, is more like it.

That's really what we're doing when we ignore what God is trying to tell us—especially when we ignore what He's been saying to us through the circumstances He's divinely allowed into our lives. We keep walking around in what we *think* is reality, although we're actually just imagining our own little version of it, the one where we're the star—the sun that all the action of life is orbiting around—feeling as if we're in full control of what we're doing, and seeing no real need for stepping off center stage.

But really—if we could honestly see what's going on— we'd recognize we're just fumbling along in the dark. We may be fooling *some* people, but we're fooling ourselves most of all. And we're not fooling God in the least.

Sleepwalking. We do it well.

And when we're in the middle of it, we never want to wake up. Not if it means loosening our grip on the freedom to call our own shots. Not if it means relinquishing control and putting our trust in His sense of direction. Not if it means we can't indulge the deceptive fantasy of being free agents who know better than anybody else how to work out this plan of ours.

And do you know what's pretty cool about God? He'll let us do that, if we insist. He'll let that be our decision. If we aren't willing to give up control to Him . . . *all right*, He'll say, *we can do it that way, if you want*.

What we *can't* decide, however, are the consequences of going ahead with that leadership style. We can't control how full or empty we'll feel once we've played out the string and done it our way. Because by deciding to live with the delusion of control, we're also deciding to limit ourselves to the finite amount of intelligence, vision, and brute strength that live inside this human body of ours—which is more than fifty percent water to start with. By the time we've splashed around and made a mess of everything with our short-sighted mistakes and misreading the warning signs, the chances of us not drowning in our own stupidity are basically slim to none. Even if people think we look like a million bucks, we'll know inside what they don't *really* know—that we're scrambling like crazy to figure out what we were supposed to be putting into these pockets of ours besides money, stuff, and things.

Look, I understand, even knowing the truth of all this, it's still a hard decision to make. To scoot out of the driver's seat. To climb down out of the high chair.

But sometimes—at what He knows is just the right time—God will spell it out for us in terms that are clearer than a Honolulu seven-day weather forecast. And when He does, He expects an answer.

If we know what's good for us, that answer had better be . . .

Surrender

I got home around 3:30 on a chilly, winter, Friday afternoon. This was about five years after Braxton was born. Barron had come along in the meantime, giving us three kids under the age of ten. In addition, after a lot of thought and prayer, we had recently started the process for adoption, working with a highly recommended agency. We were deep in the paperwork, learning the ropes of the unpredictable waiting game, hoping to bring an international child into our family sometime soon.

We had a lot going on.

But I don't know—I just felt bummed that day. January will do that to you sometimes. Early sunsets. Gray skies. Bills coming due from Christmas. A long way to go before summer vacation.

And yet what I was feeling was a lot more acute than that. Work was seeming more tedious and time-consuming than usual. Everybody wanted more of me, no matter how much I was already giving. Everything was getting bigger and harder to balance, and the pressure to keep it all up in the air without dropping something was wearing me out.

After wheeling into the driveway that afternoon, I came in through the basement door, having to kick toys out of my way just to walk through the room. And as I trudged up the stairs, one of my kids came skidding around the corner.

"Hey, Dad, look what I saw online," holding up some kind of printout of a fancy new Lego set he wanted. "Can we go to Walmart and get it tonight?"

I don't remember exactly what I said back to him. But I'm sure it had something to do with the "old" one he'd gotten from Santa Claus just the other day—and what he could do with it if he didn't like it.

Ticked me off, man.

"What's going on here?" I said to my wife, looking over to where she was standing, wondering what in the world they'd been doing all day, whatever was making them feel the need to ask me for more stuff.

"Oh, you know—"

"Well, I can tell you right now I ain't . . . never mind." (Those ungrateful little . . .)

Yeah, okay, I can say it now. Ol' Dad was in a bad mood. I'd already been in one before I pulled in the driveway. And this sneak attack with the Lego thing, well—it just caught me right in the spleen. I knew I'd better step outside before I said something else, something that would probably quiet *all* conversation for the rest of the night, possibly for the rest of the weekend.

So without even slipping my coat off, I slammed out onto the deck—our big 12-x-26 overlook that gazed across a grown man's paradise, everything a nature lover and deer hunter could want in a backyard. Frozen by the January temperatures, of course, everything had turned hard and dead and cold and brittle, but it still should've been enough to make my wife, my kids, and me just glad to be living out there. "What's the big idea, them always wanting more, more, more? Why can't they ever just be happy with what they've got?"

I was woofing pretty good.

But have you ever had one of those moments when God just kind of tells you to shut up and listen to yourself? Has a voice of reason ever kept interrupting you, even when you're trying to talk over the top of it? That's sort of what happened then. Right in the middle of my stomping and chomping about how selfish these kids of mine were growing up to be, this thought came barreling through my mind: *They're following YOU, dude!*

"What?"

Look in that barn down there! Look at the '83 Jeep in the yard. The four-wheeler, the horses, the saddles, the shotguns.

"Yeah, but that's different."

No, it's NOT different. You're a five-year-old baby, Joey, just like the one who met you at the top of the stairs a minute ago, never satisfied with what you've got.

Okay. Looked like this fresh air was making things worse, not better. I needed out of here.

And not just out on the back porch.

Stepping inside again, I said to Courtney, "Look, I'm going down to the barn. I just need to chill for a while."

"Sure," she said—because she knew, like I knew, that it wasn't just Braxton and the Lego set. It wasn't just her or the kids. It wasn't just this afternoon or the office or the house or the family. She knew I'd been stewing for at least a couple of months, saying stuff like—same as you've probably said yourself, same as you may be saying right now—"There's got to be more than this, man! I cannot keep doing this! I cannot keep going down the same old road every day to the same old place, getting the same old, same old . . ."

I'd had it. I was over it.

And I was taking it down to the barn. I muttered over my shoulder, "I'll be back."

But I *didn't* come back.

Not all that night.

Honestly, I didn't set out to set up camp for the weekend. This wasn't, like, my plan or my habit or anything. I'd never gone into the barn before to spend the night, except for a couple of times staying late down there with the boys. But on this night, I just—for whatever reason—got sucked in by the peace and quiet, and before I knew it, I'd let it get late on me, and I still didn't want to leave. I had my Bible out, had the radio off and on, had a fire going in the iron stove. I was kicked back in the hay, lulled by the soft shuffling and snorting of the horses, and thinking that some of my answers might really be hanging in the air down there if I'd just wait for them to show themselves. I don't think I'd ever been more open to hearing from God as in that moment, or more eager to figure out what to do different with this life we were living.

I faded in and out of sleep, I think, as time kept passing. Waking and sleeping sort of blended into one recurring blur. I didn't have any covers or anything, so I kept getting up to toss more wood on the fire. And despite it being no more than sixty degrees inside there, even with the flames snapping hot and steady and radiating out in all directions, I stayed reasonably comfortable . . . except for this internal gnawing inside, for more of life, and more of Him, a tangible sense that something was wrong, and that there *had* to be some way to make it right.

Dawn finally broke on Saturday morning, gleaming through the cracks and spaces in the walls, stirring me awake from a couple hours of exhausted dozing. I would spend the rest of that whole Saturday in and out of the barn, piddling around, patting the dogs, fixing stuff, hearing my kids come streaming down the hill, "Whatcha doing, Dad?"

"Aw, just hanging out."

I never went up to the house that day. I wasn't being a hermit or taking some vow of silence. I wasn't telling the kids to get out of here and leave me alone. But I wasn't ready to leave yet. I kept my coat on, kept the fire hot, kept closing the door whenever I needed to thaw out, and just kept waiting. Something—I could tell—was happening.

And at around 3:30, 4:00 that afternoon . . .

It did.

Come

As the shiver of late afternoon shadows began darkening the room, my heart slowly began churning up into what sure felt like the presence of God in there—or at least what I'd always heard and thought it would be.

Please, Lord, if it's You, please come.

Please come.

The feelings were getting thick. Intense. The verses I'd been flipping past in my Bible soon began to crackle with fire and spirit. God's promises to His people in Old Testament days suddenly started to sound like His promises to me. His challenge and demand for their complete trust and obedience began to feel like a personal appeal— as real to Joey as it had been real to Joshua. "The LORD is the One who will go before you. He will be with you; He will not leave you or forsake you. Do not be afraid or discouraged" (Deut. 31:8). I started to read what Jesus had said to His disciples, where He recalculated what their life with Him was sure to cost, but also what life with Him could surely become. "For whoever wants to save his life will lose it, but whoever loses his life because of Me will save it" (Luke 9:24). And with a level of certainty I'd never experienced before, I knew He was saying those same things to me.

Somehow unable to hold it all in, breathlessly needing to do something with these words I was reading from Scripture, I grabbed a black pen from my journal and started writing out verses on the beams and wallboards of the barn. Twenty or thirty of them. These words that were piercing my soul were now surrounding me, all around me, both in print and in power.

Unreal.

I couldn't stop. God was speaking. I could feel Him. Before I knew it, I was weeping—I'm talking about loud, unstoppable tears. Sobbing. Very un-Joey like. I wasn't being myself. And yet I wasn't about to stop God from what He was doing—because I'll tell you, I didn't *want* "myself" to be the man who came out of that barn whenever I finally got up and left. When this unusually strong experience with God was over—and I didn't care in that moment if it ever stopped—I *had* to be made of different stuff. I *had* to be changed. I *had* to be what my wife needed, what my children needed, what our future needed, most important, what He wanted and commanded of me.

It felt so peaceful to be in His presence like that—and yet it felt desperately urgent at the same time. The weight of His Word and Spirit were descending all around me, deep and established, but also young and scrappy. Like they were brand new. Alive. At times I felt like sitting perfectly still, trying not to make a sound. But then at other times I was up and pacing, gesturing, praying, worshipping, trying to talk out this full rush of truth He was blasting into my head.

It was at about this hour—long after dark, with the whole rest of the world and our house up the hill faded to black—when I started to imagine in my mind the scene I tried to describe for you at the beginning of this book. It was as if I could see myself at sixty-five, happy and settled, surrounded by all the trappings of longed-for American success. I've often thought of it since, referring to it as almost like a Scrooge moment. It wasn't exactly a vision. I'm not trying to creep you out here. But it was pretty *real* feeling. Like a Disney ride. I could see it.

And it made me sick.

"No," I said, first in a whisper, then out loud. "No. No! *No!* Don't let me go there, God! What do I do to keep from going there?"

And the answer that came back to me in the silence, reverberating in my spirit, is still scrawled in big, bold letters on those barn posts, right to this very day. Up the walls, across the beams, everywhere. SURRENDER.

Surrender.

The answer is *surrender.*

Now don't go all Stephen King on me. I wasn't having a psychotic fit, flipping out. I wasn't scratching words into the wood with my bloody fingernails. I was just pouring out and writing down what God was pouring and writing into my heart at that moment. And the only word I knew to describe it was . . . *surrender.*

Everything.

From now on.

All I've got.

All I've done.

All I am.

I'm yours, God. I surrender!

God had been with me, like He's been with you, from the moment I was born. He had watched over me and protected me and led me and cared for me all my life. So when I say He was "there" in the barn, I'm not saying He was any more present with me that night than He'd ever been before. He was a hundred percent "there" from the minute I staggered in on Friday afternoon. But by

Saturday night, He'd worn me down and cleared my head until I was a hundred percent there too. And once He got all of me focused on Him and ready to listen, He had me in a position where He knew He could talk and knew it would communicate.

I don't think moments like these can be manufactured. There's no real prescription, no step-by-step instructions that'll automatically lead you into an encounter with Almighty God. But I believe I can speak with a high level of confidence concerning at least one prerequisite: God's not likely to shoehorn important life messages into fifteen-minute time slots. We don't find out what's really on His heart by working Him in between lunch and our two o'clock. Sure, of the ten million ways we could spend ten minutes, getting alone with Him is always one of the very best options we can choose. Those are good, needed moments for reflection and resetting. But we are typically layered over with so many plans and competing thoughts, with runaway voices and squeaky distractions, the noise doesn't clear out of the room just because we shut the door.

It takes time.

He wants just *us*, not us and our carry-on baggage.

And when He finally got "just me" alone with Him that night, He basically had only one thing to say—apparently the only thing I truly needed to hear, the one thing that undoubtedly has changed everything else about my life.

Here's the way I had seen it when I went down there on Friday night. Whenever I came back out of the barn again, I was coming out to do one of two things: either I was going to chase my dreams of wealth and affluence and status and success—and do it better and faster and harder than anybody else had ever done it before—or I was pushing every last squealing brat of ambition off the cliff of faith and I was jumping off right behind 'em. I was either going to crank it all up or lay it all down.

And when Sunday came and the night finally drained away, I knew what I had to do.

Surrender.

Control Freaked

I like being in charge. I like knowing what's coming. I like taking over and doing all the delegating. I like dreaming it up and buying the equipment, planning the day's details and then showing up ready to work.

I like being the boss.

You probably do too.

Oh, maybe you're not the kind who wants to be responsible for making *all* the decisions. Maybe you don't like being the one who's on the hook for a business recommendation or even for choosing which restaurant to go to if nobody else can make up their mind. But we're all basically hesitant to let too much control get away from us. Our 12-gauges aren't the only things that'll need to be pried loose by force one day from our cold, dead hands. There's a lot more stuff we wouldn't dare give up without somebody knowing they'd been engaged in one serious fight.

We don't surrender easily.

But when it comes to how life with God goes, this battle for *control* is not a game we can win and expect to come out the better for it. Eventually each of us must come to the place where we decide who's running this show: Him or us?

Yes, you can still be a take-charge person, if that's how He's wired you to be. He won't take that temperament away from you. You're still responsible and accountable and on-the-clock for how wisely you invest yourself and your time. And no, what God does with your surrendered decision doesn't necessarily mean full-time missions or Africa or even a change of address at all. But when the switch flips in your head and your heart—the way mine did in the barn on that January weekend—we are each declaring ourselves out from under our own control. By agreeing with God about the truth of who He is and the reality of His promises toward us, we accept for ourselves the only position where we and spiritual freedom can ever reasonably show up together on the same day—the only place we'll ever experience true fullness and satisfaction.

As a passenger.

Passengers don't drive. Passengers don't work the gas, the brakes, or the steering wheel. Passengers are along for the ride but not in control of where they're going. Lord knows, of course, we can still do a lot of "driving" from the passenger seat. *Turn here, watch out, slow down, pull over. Didn't you see that? Where are you going? I should've known you'd get us lost.* But that's because we're trying to control something we were never intended to manage. And it's frustrating. It's self-defeating. It only succeeds at keeping us torqued up and out of whack, as well as all the rest of the passengers who are with us—our spouse, our children, our friends, whoever.

Good passengers just hop in. And hang on. And know that wherever God's decided to take us, He's already been there ahead of time and checked it all out for us.

When I finally appeared in the house again on Sunday afternoon, I found my wife busy in the kitchen. "Joe," she said, "I hope you've gotten what you needed to get down there, because these kids have been—"

"I know," I said, interrupting her mid-sentence, squeezing in between her and the dishwasher. I grabbed her around the waist, pulled her close to me, looked her in the eyes. And instead of telling her what I'd told her a million times before—how I was going to be better, do better, be home earlier, be more available, be more of what she needed—I just said as simply as I knew how, "Babe, as far as the direction of our journey goes, I'm afraid it's fuzzier now than it's ever been. I have no real clarity whatsoever. But what's become as clear to me as anything is this: God is in charge of our life from here on out. I mean it."

"Okay."

"I'm not asking you to say, 'Oh, that's great. That's so spiritual.' All I'm asking you for is your patience. Because

I'm telling you, I'm changed. You'll see. I'm not asking you to believe it. I'm asking you to let me prove it. From now on, Courtney . . . I am surrendered."

And if she didn't know it then, she sure knows it now.

God wrestled me to the ground in that barn. I had been telling Him for months that I wanted things to be different. I had told Him I couldn't go on doing what I was doing, not if it just ended up leaving me and my family this miserable, clueless, chaotic, and dissatisfied. And in hearing that appeal, He had made me an offer. He had shown me beyond all doubt that if I really wanted my life to change, I could do it right now. But to do so, I'd need to get off so He could get on. I'd need to step aside so He could step on the gas. I'd need to power down on my agenda and power up on His. He had come there and met me where I was, right on my property, right in my wheelhouse. But if I wanted this weekend to be more than a short-term, sugar-rush, spiritual high, then I needed to choose.

Same old, same old? Or surrender?

What'll it be?

I daresay He's asking the same thing of you.

I wish I could color this all in for you. I wish He had colored it all in for me. I sometimes wish He would draw the "You Are Here" map, and then highlight in neon marker all the routes and connection points between us and the food court, between us and the water fountain, between us and the next big attraction at the next big show time. But that's where faith comes in. That's where control is released. That's where we learn to exist without the exertion of our own pressure all the time. That's where obedience starts up and then shows what it's made of.

All of that comes later. One step at a time.

But first, for people like you and me—who are truly fed up with how empty our life feels, who have the sneaking suspicion that what we're working so hard to accomplish is ultimately bordering on irrelevant, who are certain that being a Christian cannot possibly be as thin and bland and pointless as ours has turned out to be—it starts with one basic choice.

And all I know is this, from my own personal experience.

He had me at surrender.

Chapter 3

Obedience Is Not a Process

"Franklin Businessman Turns South African Farmer," read the profile article in our hometown newspaper. I got a real kick out of that when I saw it, because while my current ministry assignment does involve running a vegetable-growing operation (I'll tell you more about that later), I'm still about the furthest thing from being a farmer there is. The Lord has led me to a wonderful team of knowledgeable, hardworking people with amazing agricultural smarts and skills. Me, on the other hand—I can hardly keep my bushes alive.

In fact, one of the first orders of "farming" business I undertook when we arrived in country had very little to do with plants in the ground, but rather the relocation of two freestanding greenhouses. We needed to transport them to our ministry campus from a plot of land four miles away.

Each greenhouse (or *tunnel*, as they're called in South Africa) was about 8-x-30 meters—roughly 25 feet by 100 feet. Big structures. You don't just back up a flatbed, hoist them up, and haul them off. Maybe in America you would, but not here. The roads aren't the best, the trucks aren't the biggest, and the risk of hurting somebody or breaking something is much too high. There was no real way to do a wide-load transfer from that spot.

So here's what we did instead. Starting in late November, we conducted a meticulous inventory of both units, labeling every panel and piece of hardware with permanent marker. Everything got a number. Bolt-1. Bar-2. T-3. I drew the whole thing out on a pad—like an exploded diagram—corresponding to the code I'd assigned to each individual component. Then once everything had been tagged and double-checked, we began slowly dismantling the tunnels one at a time, piece by piece.

I'll bet I made a hundred trips, easy—four miles there, four miles back—usually with just a piece of plastic and three metal bars of connecting supports in tow. I'd laugh with the guys sometimes, telling them I could've carried this whole thing in one or two loads if I'd been driving my three-quarter-ton pickup, the one I'd owned back in the States. I don't think they ever believed me. But by the time we'd lugged those tunnels to their new location in dozens of shifts, and after putting them back together as carefully as we'd taken them apart, the project had eaten up nearly three full months of hot southern hemisphere summer, stopping only for Christmas. (I know it's weird, but that's how our seasons work.) I could still break out in a sweat just thinking about it. What an undertaking!

It was a *process*, let me tell you. For certain tasks, that's the only way you can do it.

But not with obedience.

Obedience is not a process.

Obedience is simply a *now*.

When God burned His Word into my soul that weekend in the barn, when He peeled back the narrow opening of "surrender" for me to walk through—and gave me no other specifics for how this path was going to work itself out—He wasn't asking me to set up a meeting to discuss it later. He wasn't using the heat from my fire pit to warm me up to the idea, hoping maybe we could schedule a future weekend here in a few months to consider the matter more in-depth.

The plans and implications for how this life change was supposed to happen would come together in due time. *His* time. But the moment and mind-set of surrender—on my part—was supposed to be immediate. Done. Go. Do it.

Surrender comes first.

And everything after that? That's God's business.

I'm not saying we're supposed to disengage all common sense when we turn complete control of our planning systems over to Him. The Bible, when it speaks of rashness, puts it within the overall category of foolishness. Stupidity. God commends the man who seeks counsel from others, who does his homework, who applies careful, patient thought and wisdom to where he's going with his future. Nothing wrong with using your head. That's good business. Even for spiritual business.

Because, yes, when God starts doing what He wants to do with us, there's a process at work. He takes us from place to place, from person to person, from one opportunity to the next. One thing builds on another. We grow. We mature. We progress from experience to experience.

But surrender and obedience are not like that. They're what you might think of as the wall switches of faith. If we want to be able to see the next step where this path of His is taking us, we can't just be nudging and poking around and sort of looking into the idea of going along with Him on this. We can't be open to it only on those every-so-often Sunday mornings when the preaching is particularly good. Nobody who expects to see inside a dark room just sits there and tries not to touch the light switch, or to move it as little as they can.

No, we throw it. We flip it.

We're in. We're on.

Let's do this.

Obedience.

Surrender.

That's all the process there is to it.

Blasting Off-Ramps

You'll remember Paul's encounter with Jesus on the road to Damascus (Acts 9). Knocked the guy to the ground. Blew his tires out. Blistered him all the way to the back of his eyeballs. Like me in the barn, he knew he had experienced a "moment" with God—and he sure didn't confuse it as an invitation to coffee.

"Get up and go into the city," Jesus told him. *Just do it. That's all you need to worry about. And once you've done that, once you're there,* "you will be told what you must do" (Acts 9:6). The only place where Paul (Saul) was going to receive any answers, any instructions, or any form of itinerary for his future was in Damascus. And the only way he was getting to Damascus was by going there. By obeying. By surrendering to what really was a very basic, very simple command: "Get up and go."

I think we all experience moments like these—times when we know we need to do something, when God clears away the clutter and makes plain what He's both offering us and expecting of us. Unlike those common, everyday tweaks on our conscience, unlike those ordinary times of prayer when we do all the talking and aren't really interested in listening, these kind of moments are unmistakable. If not dramatic, at least obvious. We know what He's saying. We know this is big. We know we're at a spiritual crossroads—we're either getting in, or we're getting out. But either way, we're making a choice.

Surrender, or not.

Be His, or don't.

Obey, or do it your own stupid way.

There are no trial-size bottles of obedience. No little pink Baskin-Robbins spoons where you can test to see if you think the Rocky Road is really worth reaching into your wallet for. When God is calling you, when you know He wants all of you, and you know you're hesitant about making so bold a move, especially when you don't have a clue where it all might lead—

I'm just telling you, the freedom and joy and spiritual passion and life mission that you crave (and God makes possible, for the sake of His great name) is exactly what that decision will either cost you or make real for you.

It's not a process.

It's a switch flip.

And there's a reason for that.

Honestly, we ought to be self-aware enough by now to know that if we only commit to sticking our toe in, gauging the temperature under various conditions, getting back with Him in a week or ten days to let Him know what we're thinking, we'll never stick this out. We'll always go back to the places where we feel safer and more at home, where we make sure we're taking care of ourselves first.

And that's why, when I came out of the barn on Sunday evening, I said to myself, "Joey, man, this surrender thing starts bright and early Monday morning." Because I *knew* what God had said. I *knew* like never before what my commitment level to Him was supposed to entail. And I *knew* if I left myself access to enough off-ramps—enough ripcords, enough emergency exits—I would find a way before very long to work back to where I'd come from. If the only change I brought with me out of the barn was a change of perspective but not an immediate change of lifestyle, then there wasn't going to be any change at all. I mean, there never had been much change *before*. What would happen if I ever told people what had happened to me, but I still looked like the exact same person I'd always been? Why should I expect anybody to believe me? Or to care? Or to notice?

So on Monday morning, I got up.

And started selling stuff.

Whatever they were charging for it on Craigslist, that's what I asked. And if somebody didn't want to pay that much? Fine. Name your price. So the four-wheeler? Gone. The Jeep? Gone. The horses and the horse trailer? Gave them away. They're in Colorado now. Probably loving it. We gave away two purebred German shepherds, sold my zero-turn Toro mower, and watched our furniture walk right out of the living room. It was like a regular Joey's Bargain Barn.

Does that mean if you don't start liquidating all your assets and selling the house from under your feet, you're not surrendered to God? I can't tell you that. When Jesus told the rich young ruler to "sell all you have and give to the poor, and you will have treasure in heaven" (Mark 10:21), He wasn't making a blanket statement for everybody. He just knew what was inside the heart of that particular man. He knew what was keeping that one guy from truly following, just like he knew where *my* idols were and what was keeping me all locked up inside myself, where I couldn't experience Him full in the face because of all the stuff that was propped up in between us.

But I can tell you this—when total surrender to God starts showing up in your habits, in your calendar, in your checkbook, in your schedule, in your family life, in your marriage, in your time commitments, you don't need to go around preaching to people about the difference Jesus makes. No longer is your personal testimony just a bunch of churchy-sounding words. It looks like real life. And it communicates in real time.

Your surrender may look different from mine. But it can't just be a 10-percent adjustment or investment, amortized over a period of years.

It's not a process.

Or else it doesn't hold a lot of promise.

Be Afraid, Be Very Afraid

I don't know if you're tracking with me or not. You may just think I'm crazy. I'd understand that. (Probably am.) Like I said at the first, I don't expect everybody to want what I'm talking about here, and I don't expect *anybody* not to feel resistant about turning loose from the normal attachments and cuddle bears we've always clung to.

Life is a constant buildup of expectations and desires that we accept without really questioning. With all the needs and insecurities rattling around inside us, we spend the bulk of our energy—both intentionally and subconsciously—looking for sources of refuge, places where we feel accepted, people who help us feel good about our-selves, possessions that make us feel safe and confident and at rest. That's why we want our retirement account maxed out, if we can. That's why we want the kids' col-lege plans funded in advance. That's why we want the good job and benefits and the termite protection on the house. And if something or somebody comes along to mess with that—even if it's God Himself—look, we're just barely hanging on as it is, so don't go making us any more unsteady and unsettled and uncomfortable than we already feel.

I get that. I do.

Surrender scared me too. Scared me to death, actually.

Still does, actually.

For weeks and months after that incredible experi-ence with God, there were so many times when I ques-tioned what I was doing. All I needed (and truly wanted sometimes) was for my wife to say, "Joey, I think you've lost your mind. We can't do this. Come on." That might have been all it took. That way I could have blamed my disobedience on her. How convenient. Because being surrendered had the potential for costing me (and us) everything. Believe me, I could feel a hundred thousand little threads pulling hard against my forward momen-tum, tugging me backwards with everything from worry and family and friends to prestige and trajectory and nos-talgia—anything you can imagine. Anything that would make me stop and get a grip. *What are you THINKING, man? Where are you going with this?*

I still didn't know. I had no answer for that question. That part would need to be a process.

But every morning would need to be *surrender*.

That's all I knew.

It got so conflicting, so tempting, so easy to want to forget, I finally wrote the word "Surrender" on a sticky note and pressed it against the mirror in our bathroom. Every morning when I'd brush my teeth, every time I checked my shirt and hair to see how I looked, and every night when I'd step back in there before bed after a long day, I was forcing myself not to be able to shake the one thing, the *only* thing, God had said He wanted from me.

My obedient surrender.

That word and that decision became my new refuge. Where stuff and salary and persona had been my refuges of choice before, I was choosing now to cut all ties with any man-made links to safety and importance. Like the Bible says, I was making the *Lord* "my refuge," trusting the promise that "He will give His angels orders concerning you, to protect you in all your ways" (Ps. 91:9–11).

Part of me was wanting to bail out and go back. Another part of me was itching to firm this up into a battle plan that I could see and prepare for. But God just wanted me surrendered. He just wanted me running to Him for refuge. And if I would do that—even when it was a struggle, sometimes daily, sometimes *hourly*—He would take care of the rest.

I just had to keep hoping that He would take care of the rest.

Something I Need to Tell You

One of the hardest conversations pending as a result of what God was doing in my life was the talk I needed to schedule with my parents. This wasn't going to be easy.

I was the leader of my dad's company—actually, *our* company at the time since I'd become a part owner. I had taken on responsibilities for him so that he could go do other things. And if I was suddenly to tell him that maybe I was relinquishing the role I'd been performing for him, it would obviously carry a personal impact. I wasn't just running a potential risk to his grandchildren's safety. I was telling him something that might significantly change his private plans for the next few months to a year.

So this was daunting.

My decision—this crazy decision—was affecting a lot of people. Not just me.

We met, my mom and dad and I, at a woodsy-looking barbecue place on the main drag. It's built to be all home-style and comfort food, but I can assure you my stomach was in a twisted knot of pulled pork perplexity. I don't think I've ever been as nervous in my whole life—oh, maybe when a bunch of us used to go cliff diving in the dark at a nearby rock quarry, sixty-foot drops. But, boy, I'd have taken the feeling of my swimming trunks riding up to my ears rather than what was churning inside me at that restaurant booth. I didn't know how they were going to react or how I was going to describe it.

You may have noticed by now I'm a pretty straightfor-ward guy. And even in being unusually ill at ease that day,

I finally just launched in and said to my dad, before we'd really dug in to our sandwiches good, "There's no other way to say this: I feel like God is calling me to do something different. I don't know exactly what it is yet—missions maybe? I don't really know. I just know He's telling me to surrender, to let Him lead me on a new path."

Whoo.

Silence.

"And I know, Dad, this is probably flooring you. *You? Joey? A missionary? You kidding me?* Plus, I know that what I'm telling you has implications for the business. Big ones. But from where I'm sitting right now and with what I'm sensing and thinking . . . I've *got* to get out. I need to start executing whatever plan that God is wanting to establish with us. And I know this is hard to take, but I hope you understand where I'm coming from."

I think, as I remember back on it, my gaze must have sunk lower and lower the longer I'd kept talking. Maintaining eye contact was a struggle. But when I reached the end and had laid the guts of my little speech out on the table there, I looked up to see how it had landed. And my dad—my John Wayne dad—

He was crying.

I'd never seen that before. Ever. Shocking.

So in the several seconds that passed while he was looking at me, then looking over at my mom, who by that time had started crying herself, I wasn't sure how I was supposed to interpret this. Was he furious? Was he crushed? Was he worried sick? What was it?

"Son," he said, finally getting some words out, "uh, you don't know this, but, um . . . I've been fasting and praying every Wednesday for the past year. And I've had two things on my list of prayer requests from the very beginning: (1) that God would call one of you boys to be a pastor, and (2) that He would call one of my kids into foreign missions.

"And, no, I never thought it would be you!"

We all laughed at that. Of course. Broke the tension.

"I was thinking it would be Gavin or Taylor," he said, one of my brothers, "certainly not the head of my business. But I believe you've heard from the Lord, son. And I fully support what you're doing.

"And I'm very, very proud of you."

(Whew—I'm crying again right now.)

But that's why, with God, obedience is not a process decision. It's not something we can wait on, delaying it until He comes out and shows us everything He intends to do with it. We can't play Him that way. He's not fooled by that.

But once He has us—once He has our complete obedience, our full surrender—man, He will plunk us into such an ocean of sovereign, exciting activity, this little gourd on our shoulders can't even deal with it.

My dad—did you hear what I said?—my dad, unbeknownst to me, had felt the tug of God and had been obedient to Him for a full year's time, praying a very specific prayer that, as it turns out, was specifically for me! How could I have pulled that off myself?

And what if I had gagged on God's call to surrender? What if I had told Him to show me what He really meant by that, and then I'd think about it? How many more years of frustration would my dad have kept on investing in that prayer before giving up and deciding he must've just heard wrong from God after all? What do you think my confession that afternoon did to his faith? What kind of confidence did God grow in my father's heart when he heard it?

I can tell you the confirmation it gave to *me*. I felt like a dog turned loose from his pen. Get out of my way, I'm *going!* I'm *free!* I couldn't believe it. This was really happening. The greatest blessing God could possibly have given me in that moment, second only to the loving support of my dear wife, was the prayerful blessing of my parents. And wouldn't you know it—He had poured it out stronger and richer on me than I could ever have imagined.

And, oh—just as a sidebar—I don't mind admitting that one other result of all this activity was the future growth and success of our family business. My brother Nathan and brother-in-law Richard have taken charge of it and are accomplishing more with it now than I ever could. I inadvertently, just in trying to do my best, had been sort of stifling some of our business potential, keeping us from expanding to fill more needs and to work more effectively. There were things I hadn't seen and hadn't thought about. But as I look at that situation today, I just consider it the passed-along blessings of an obedient life. It's just what God does.

He fills up my kids, my wife, and me until—seriously, I don't think we could possibly be any more full and fulfilled and rocked out with God's blessings than we are today. And yet instead of just topping us off, filling up *our* empty spaces, He lets the blessings of obedience run over the edge until other people around us are sloshing in it too, just as we're benefiting from the blessings of their faithfulness and trust as well.

It's incredible.

"To obey is better than sacrifice," the Bible says (1 Sam. 15:22). Brother, you've got *that* right. Whatever amount of perceived loss and cost appears to be drained from our account whenever we throw ourselves full bore into God's program, we're actually just pouring gas on a spiritual fire. We're handing Him the keys, and He's driving us to places we didn't even know existed.

And we thought He was asking too much of us, just by asking us to obey Him.

That joke's on us.

And if we're not willing to go there, it's not very funny.

His Process, Not Ours

God is so faithful. He's so loving. He knows us so well.

He knows, for example, that we need peace. Are you at peace today? With where you are? With what you're doing? If you're not, then why not? Why do you think so? Where have you been expecting your sense of peace and stability to come from? From a better job? From bigger accomplishments? From the next big thrill?

"You," the prophet Isaiah said of God, "will keep the mind that is dependent on You in perfect peace, for it is trusting in You" (Isa. 26:3). When He invites us into full dependence toward Him, into total trust, into utter obedience and surrender, He's really just inviting us into peace—the only place where peace on earth is actually found and kept. In Him. *Completely* in Him.

I'll never forget how the peace of surrender washed over me one day in, of all places, a mall parking lot. A twenty-seven-year-old kid from Kentucky had driven down with a friend to close the deal on buying my truck—my beautiful, beloved Chevy Silverado 4x4 with the Duramax diesel engine, fully tricked out with every bell and whistle you could put on it. I promise you, the only way I'd ever envisioned unloading that vehicle was to trade it in for something even bigger and better. But instead, here I was—tossing the keys into a perfect stranger's fist and preparing to watch him drive off in it.

Bummer.

He had already deposited $25,000 into my bank account. The only thing left was the $5,000 balance contained inside the white envelope he handed me as we made the exchange. We shook hands. He climbed inside. And off he went.

And since Courtney appeared to be a little late coming to pick me up, I was sort of stranded there for a while. No car. No ride. No way to get home.

And amazingly, unexpectedly, I felt so incredibly . . . good.

Like, *I feel better now.*

"What's with this feeling, God?" I said almost out loud. I really wasn't expecting this—this peace.

But, see, He knew when the time was right for me to watch my big ol' truck revving out of the parking lot toward McDonald's, then out of my life forever, and for me to see this transfer of title as a . . . as a good thing.

Putting it up for sale had been immediate. No process at all. Surrender. But orchestrating the deal so that it came down on this day, at this time, at this stage of my life journey with Him—God did that for *me*. He knew I wasn't ready eight months before, six months before, three months before, maybe three *weeks* before. But He knew that my obedience had been achieving a tangible effect on my heart and my attitudes. And so when I was left there with nothing but my shoes for transportation, He had already gone ahead and made sure I was amply filled from head to toe at that very moment . . . with peace.

His desire is for us to experience His peace. Which is what you'd think we'd want too. So I don't know why we prefer our physical, mental, emotional, and spiritual exhaustion instead. I guess we just think peace will finally appear one of these days if we keep working at it long enough, if we muscle through.

But you know good and well it won't. There's no process that leads us to peace and satisfaction, to lasting security and contentment. We don't have the goods for accomplishing those things. All we can really offer up in that direction is our obedience and surrender, our trust that He and His Word are telling us the truth—our faith, our belief, and the changes in lifestyle that flow out of it.

The rest is His.

And trust me, He knows what to do with it—because He knows *you*. And He knows me. He knows what we're ready for and what we're not. He knows what we can stand (and knows it's a lot more than we think). But He also knows what peace and joy and freedom and real love would look like if they were flowing through us and coming out of us.

And thank God that He never stops working to lead us there, despite the fact that we're so ignorant and resistant at knowing what's truly best for us.

Our life today in South Africa is filled with as many uncertainties as ever. Being faithful to His call, even to the point of quitting my job and moving my family halfway around the world, has not given me an exemption from waking up every morning with the one-focus mission of being obedient and surrendered. That's still the only way I know how to roll—the only way that doesn't leave me buried in worry and panicked about the future—the only way that I'm assured is taking me to the places I really and truly want to go.

Yeah, we're a long way deep into this process now. But obedience is still not a process. Not for me, not for you. It starts fresh today. It'll start fresh again tomorrow.

And whether we like it or not, that's what changes the water line on the half-empty life.

Somewhere in the late spring, early summer of 2009—after we had made our intentions known about preparing to go on the mission field, yet were still nowhere close to realizing the wheres or whens or anything concrete at all—I joined a bunch of guys on a construction trip to Nicaragua, same as we had done the year before.

The first time had been a real shock to my system. I'd never seen poverty and desperation on that kind of level. Horrifying, heartbreaking stuff. But the second time, coming four or five months on the heels of my experience with God in the barn, and draped in the understanding that missions for me would no longer be just a ten-day excursion with a bunch of fun-loving guys anymore, I looked at Nicaragua quite a bit differently on that follow-up trip.

I remember being in the bus once we got there, riding out to the camp where we'd be staying for the week. Bumpy. Backwards. Hot. Smelly. At some point, the leader stood up—good friend of mine—and was talking to everybody, giving instructions and so forth. Then pointing at me, he said, "Joey's here with us again, but this will be his last time. He and his family are going to the mission field."

Courtney's dad was on this trip too. That made it more personal than ever. I looked over and saw the tears in his eyes as Brent was making that statement. And the reality of it all came swooping around my shoulders and weighing me down hard in that clankety, uncomfortable seat. "It's surreal, guys," I said, "to be riding here through a third-world country, knowing that in eight or nine months, a year maybe, a place like this could be my home."

Nobody said anything. Just the roar of the bus, and the roar of thoughts in my head.

Finally I broke the silence, risking claim to my man card. "I'll be honest with you, boys, I'm scared to death."

The roar kept sounding as my voice trailed off.

"Scared to death . . ."

Yep, and like I mentioned before, I still get scared sometimes even today. It's not easy. And I know your life isn't easy either, or any less scary than mine in a whole lot of ways. But of all the things I might be scared about, nothing scares me more than living outside God's will. Nothing terrifies me more painfully than the thought of living depleted by my own independence, living inside the same house with all my possessions but without any real purpose to go along with them.

That's scary to me. After seeing what I've seen, after experiencing life out in the open with God, I'd die if I wasn't surrendered to this and to Him, if I'd been unwilling to trust Him to take care of my future and my family. All He asks is our obedience. What a small price to pay for His presence.

Get up. And go do it.

Chapter 4

When Even Christians Think You're Crazy

The missions pastor at our church, Scott Harris, looked across his desk at me, and did what missions pastors are sometimes called on to do: test the witness.

"So let me get this straight," he said, "your life's pretty much okay?"

"Yeah."

"Nothing's wrong? There's nothing you'd want to tell me?"

"No, we're good. Seriously."

"You're not in financial trouble?"

"No."

"Not having marriage problems?"

"No."

"Haven't lost your job?"

"No—I mean, well, yeah, but I'm losing it on purpose, not because I *have* to."

He looked back at me in silence, waiting for the revelation, the real motive—why the sudden change in plans and life direction. He'd been telling me for six weeks, ever since I went to see him to talk about the tug I was feeling toward missions, that I needed to keep praying about it, to be thinking about it, let's commit this to the Lord. So, okay, that's what we did. But now I was back. In his office. And I wasn't changing my story.

"No, my life is perfect, Scott. If there's a problem, *that's* the problem. It's perfect. *Too* perfect."

I'd been able to see it now. Our perfect life just wasn't so perfect anymore. The cloud of dust we'd been kicking up every day to keep this family-of-five operation up to speed had been blown away by a chilly gust of reality. And what it revealed as the haze began to clear was a hamster with my same build and haircut, running like mad on a squeaky wheel, discovering to my stunned amazement that I was trapped in a cage I hadn't even noticed before. And the pitiful part was, it would *always* be like that, no matter how many spins I took on that workout equipment, no matter how fast and furiously I kept it up.

I don't know what that realization would feel like if it ever dawned on a hamster. But I sure know what it felt like to me. *It stunk!* "So, yeah, man, something's wrong. I don't know exactly what you'd call it, but God's told me I need to fix it. And missions, I believe, is part of how that's supposed to happen."

"All right then," he said, seeming convinced by my answers that I wasn't running from the law or anything. "Let's start talking about next steps."

And you know what? I'm thankful for people like that—like Scott Harris—brothers who can handle testimonies like mine with discernment, who know that if God is truly at work in a person's heart, He'll keep His calling in force. It's smart of people, when they're trying to help us, to check and see if the pilot light stays on, to find out if the intrusion of daily life has diluted the conviction and calling we'd been talking so much about at first.

There's wisdom in that.

But whatever we decide to do after this kind of watchfulness and prayer, one thing's for sure: it can't be to do nothing. God doesn't waste His breath on us just to liven up a worship service. When He gets your attention, when He exposes the ugly backside of your hidden idols, when He shines a spiritual light on where this spinning-wheel lifestyle of yours is actually taking you, He may not be steering you all the way to a foreign mission field, but He's sure not sending you back to bed either. He wants *something*—something that He knows is for your ultimate good and for the kingdom connections He wants to make through you.

And if you actually did it—whatever that "something" is—I can guarantee you it'd probably shock a few people.

Even Christian people.

Like maybe your spouse. Or some of your clients, coworkers, and employees. Maybe even your pastor or Sunday school teacher or some of your friends who talk such a big game at church.

That's because unspoken standards are in place that determine what goes for approved Christian behavior. You can take it to a certain level and expect to be thought of as a fine person, a spiritual model. Good dude. Take it much *past* that point, however, and you're teetering on being labeled a spiritual freak job. People might think you've gone a little crazy.

I'll say it again—even Christian people.

So with this being the case, how willing are you to go there? Out there? Beyond the edges of normal and respectable? Past the customary limits of what's admired in a good churchgoer? Out where people might actually start to worry about you a little bit, feel the need to pull you back from the edge, talk you down from the ladder, wonder what's motivating you to do what you're doing?

Would you do something bold that God was stirring inside you, even if half the people in your life didn't understand it? Would you let that stop you? Would you let *anything* stop you if you knew it was likely to put you smack in the center of God's perfect plan for your life?

Is it really so crazy to want that?

Don't Let It Hit You

I can't explain it, but we just went ahead and did it. Along with selling our stuff and thinning down our obligations, I began a swift but methodical severance transition away from active leadership in our company. Just walked away. Big step. Within a little more than six months, the plan we developed would keep me on reduced salary for continued service to the business while we worked on getting the immediate future of our family to gel into some kind of shape. In the meantime, we signed up with a missionary agency, who paired us with a consultant to walk us through the process, and we started to feel nervously excited about where all this new activity might be taking us. We had no idea where, just surrender. The only thing I thought I knew was that after everything I'd chosen to lay on the line, after the way I'd flung open the barn door for God to take complete control over us and our future, I expected all the other doors to just come flying open as well.

That's what your Christian mind and your Christian friends will tell you. You pray that if you're following His lead, God will open the doors of opportunity and direction, and that He'll close them if you're not. We think that's how we determine if we're on the right track. That's what people are supposed to see happening to us, and then go, "Oh, wow, good—I guess that's working out for 'em after all. Cool."

But what about when that's *not* what happens?

What about when the doors slam shut? What then?

Very shortly into our time line of surrender and selling stuff and signing off on some serious bottom lines, a letter arrived in the mail from our missions organization, offering their cordial regrets and apologies, but saying that due to a lack of funding, all short-term assignments (like ours was supposed to be) were being suspended for the time being, and they didn't say for how long.

To which I said . . . huh?

You mean we're being told no? They don't have a place for us?

For a want-to-be missionary? Are you kidding me?

Okay, wait, they do realize I'm volunteering here, right? I wasn't actually applying for a job opening. I was just making my plans known and trying to go through the right channels. I mean, they do remember I'm in the middle of unraveling a well-paying career to do this, that I'll be left standing on the outside looking in by the close of summer. And I don't have a fallback. Or half my furniture anymore. Help me understand.

Truth is—just being gut-level honest with you here—I think if I hadn't already begun selling off a sizable chunk of our worldly goods, there's a strong chance I'd have actually been *relieved* to get that letter. If that door had closed in my face a couple of months earlier in the game, I might have thought, "Well, hey, we tried, didn't we? What's a guy supposed to do? If they won't take me, then I can't very well go. Call up the condo place, babe—summer vacation's back on!"

But at this point . . . no sir, this wasn't gonna work. I mean I could relate to the problem they were having. Tough economy and all. I'm sure they were dealing with things the best they could. But me—I was going to the mission field. No letter in any mailbox was changing any of that.

The only thing it was changing was my naïve view of God and of faith and surrender—the kind that says if we give Him what He wants, He'll push all the clearance buttons and signature stamps and grant us smooth sailing and passage from there on in.

No, what He wants is our heart. Our loyalty. Our trust. And sometimes the only place we can truly give those to Him is at the threshold of a closed door.

And He knows it.

So will that be the end of our surrender? Is that as far as we'll push our faith? Will the first or second brick wall we face be enough to make us back off entirely and decide, y'know, we might've been a little hasty to try something this far out of our control and comfort zone? After all, what's so wrong with just being a good person and doing the best we can, pasting Scripture verses on our blog and keeping a Bible on our desk? What's the point in overdoing it? People seem to look up to us just fine the way we are, don't they?

But I think the better questions to ask ourselves go something like this: If I walk away from this closed door, will it make me feel spiritually free and confident? Will it lead me toward the kind of fulfillment and purpose and relevance I've been craving? If I let this obstacle send me back to my old normal, what are the chances my new normal will look any different five years from now than it does today? What if the normal I really want for myself and my family is only available to us on the other side of that closed door?

African Rescue

God had actually been teaching us about closed doors for quite a while. If you've ever tried to adopt, you know how events can speed up and slow down, how just when you feel like you know what's coming next and how long it should take, you realize you don't really know anything at all. Too many details in play. Too many things can happen.

Adoption was something we always felt God leading us toward. We actually anticipated as a young couple—if God chose to give us children—that we would one day add to our family by reaching out to bring an orphan into our home, or as many as He might want to give us. We were serious about that.

So pretty soon after Barron was born, we began taking some official steps toward investigating the possibility. And when they laid out the materials in front of us, as we started to imagine what country we might want to pursue as the source of our adoption, Courtney and I both felt drawn toward Vietnam. The plight of the orphans there was serious, and it just seemed like the right match for us. So we paid for the profile, got into the system, went through the home studies and interviews and finger-printing and all, and finally received the notice that our application for international adoption had been approved by the U.S. department that handles those things: CIS— Citizenship and Immigration.

But no sooner were we cleared to add our name to the waiting list . . . than the waiting list closed down. Suspicions of corruption and child trafficking had halted all adoptions coming out of Vietnam to America, and while the two governments tried to come to workable terms, we tried coming to grips with what this turn of events meant for us.

The easiest thing to do at that point was to quit. We'd expended a lot of time and effort and emotional energy, not to mention forking over a good sum of money, and apparently it had all amounted to nothing. Nobody could fault us for not trying, and it wasn't like our family wasn't bustling and complete enough with the three kids we already had.

But did God have *us*? Did He have our hearts?

And had He brought us to a closed door to find out?

About a month of hard praying later, we learned that one of the countries where 100 percent of our invested money could roll into, without being forfeited, was Ethiopia. At that, Courtney started doing some deep fact-finding, and discovered a shocking list of statistics that broke her heart—things like, how one in six Ethiopian children die before their fifth birthday, how hundreds of thousands are orphaned there by AIDS parents, how half the children never attend school and are ravaged by malnutrition.

And yet this open door toward Ethiopia had brought me to another closed door—a door I had closed myself.

I'm sorry, I just wasn't ready to have a black baby. I know it's an awful thing to say—it's an even worse way to feel—but trust me, I knew people who would not be happy with me if I brought an African child into our family. I could just imagine the looks we were going to get and the questions we were going to be asked and the whispers we were likely to hear (and not hear).

Just didn't seem like a good idea.

So, what about it, Joey? Are you surrendered to Me? Is this where it stops for you—your trust, your faith, your openness to what I've got for you?

I can tell you right now, I could not be any more crazy than I am today for this little Ethiopian girl God gave to us. The people who cared for her at the orphanage had tagged her as being "serious" and "grave" in demeanor, even as just a tiny six- or eight-month-old. But almost from the moment she climbed into my wife's smiling arms, and felt the tears of a mother's pure love against her face, she has been like a gleaming shaft of energy and sunlight. One laugh and one look from her eyes, and I am gone. I don't even want to imagine life without her being part of our family.

I could not be more proud to be her daddy.

And I'd feel the same way even if we'd never left the States.

But to have her here now in the context of South Africa, she is not just Bristol Lankford, the one from that family who adopted the little black girl. She makes us like a walking, talking picture of the gospel, everywhere we go.

If you think race relations in the American South, 150 years after the Civil War, are still tinged with certain generational biases, you should try the culture in South Africa sometime, where they're only a few decades removed from apartheid. If you can imagine in your head some of the parking lot glances we'd probably get in my hometown of Dickson, Tennessee, if our biracial family were to climb out of the car, multiply those stares and head spins by about twenty-five or thirty—or fifty—and you're maybe getting close to the feel of Cape Town in broad daylight. The sight of seeing us walking together down the street can cramp people up a good bit.

But with Bristol holding my hand as my daughter, I don't look like just another big ol' fat, white missionary from America over here to save the poor Africans from themselves. By taking one of their own into my home for keeps, they can see in a heartbeat that I truly love and respect them as a people. We're not just another white family, like many of the others here, still inclined to treat blacks like they're less than equals. Nothing quite communicates God's love in South Africa like a white father adopting a black child and giving her the same kind of affection as all my other kids get from me.

We turned the knob on a closed door to go save a little girl from Africa, and God opened it wide enough to rescue me and my heart as well—to bring me *to* Africa—where He could turn me loose to serve Him and where He would satisfy and fulfill my life in ways I never saw coming.

And it all started at a closed door.

When One Door Closes . . .

"I'm glad you don't look too devastated by the news," Scott Harris told me when I went to ask him about what that letter meant.

"Devastated?"

"Yeah, you know . . ."

"No, I'm not devastated. I just want to see what to do next."

"Well, we can probably look into some training, I think."

"Sure, good, but . . . what about going on the mission field? That's what I'm here to do, right? I came here to go on the mission field."

"Right. Right," he said, leaning back in his chair, trying to think what to do with a guy like me, who apparently didn't know a stop sign from a green light. Then after a deep breath, he said, "Tell you what, Joey, I've got an idea for you. Have you ever heard of Living Hope?"

"Living Hope . . ." I said, slowly, trying to think where I'd heard that name before. "Oh, yeah, Living Hope. They show a video about them sometimes on the screen in church. Yeah, yeah. South Africa. I'm pretty sure I gave some money to them last year."

"Right, we've partnered with them and try to help support them through the church. I happen to know they've recently started a job creation platform as part of their ministry. I don't know exactly what all it entails, and like I said, they're still in the early stages."

"Hmm, okay." Of course I didn't know anything about it yet, but just the sound of it had an interesting ring to it. *Job creation.* That's something I actually halfway understood.

"In fact," Scott said, "the guy who started Living Hope—John Thomas, and his wife, Avril—are scheduled to be here in a couple of weeks. What about if we set up a meeting for you and Courtney to sit down with them, just to hear him tell you what they're doing, let him hear what God's been doing with you—see how the Lord might lead."

Well, that sounded like some action.

And action is all I wanted.

But little did I know how much action was about to spark from that one meeting—and how it would ignite our whole life into a Spirit-fed, global adventure.

We met outside on the veranda at our church, just the four of us. Beautiful spring day. And after hearing me give the semi-short version of my testimony and some background on what I'd been doing in business, John looked back at me with tears in his eyes, and said (in that beautiful South African accent of his), "I don't expect you to know what all this means, Joey, but I've been praying for you for three years. And I truly believe we could use you in our ministry."

Well, if I *didn't* understand, then I wasn't paying attention. Sounds like God had been talking to *him* just like He'd been talking to my *dad*.

More confirmation by the moment.

John, a South African pastor—a white man—had been gripped from early on in his life about the racial injustices that were once prevalent within governmental policy, by the impoverished living conditions of many of the blacks in his country, and by the ravages of HIV and AIDS that were decimating whole lives and families. Living Hope, which had begun as a very organic, broken-hearted outreach based out of his own church, became in 2000 an established, independent ministry, reaching people for Christ by reaching into some of the cruelest pockets of poverty and disease you'll ever see in your life.

As God blessed their work, the ministry grew, until the city of Cape Town—seeing the effectiveness of their efforts—arranged for them to rent a $3 million college campus complex for less than $100 a year, for the purpose of developing an economic empowerment program focused on education and job creation. In the three years after beginning this arm of their ministry (called Living Way), those who led and served there had been accomplishing some amazing results through teaching and practical business opportunities, through uplifting people's skill levels and earning potentials. But as we sat together in the church courtyard that afternoon, John said, "What we're needing now is an entrepreneur who can come in and work with us to take it to the next level.

"And I believe," he said, "you might be that person."

I looked at Courtney. She looked at me.

This was definitely going to need some prayer, but I was seriously intrigued.

"Have you ever heard of Hannibal Smith?" John asked me.

"*Heard* of him?" (The only thing that surprised me then—and still surprises me now, knowing John the way I've gotten to know him—is that *he'd* ever heard of him!) "Sure, I've heard of him. *The A-Team.*"

He nodded, laughing. "That's what's running through my head, sitting here today—what Hannibal Smith used to say—'I love it when a plan comes together!'"

And just to think—it all started with a rejection letter.

Stack of Stones

We didn't know where this was going. John Thomas obviously seemed to indicate the door was open, and his words grew more encouraging every time I replayed them in my mind. But a lot of things still stood between us and this South African opportunity. For all practical purposes, the door was only *cracked* open, not *standing* open.

And as Courtney and I stood there in the days and weeks that followed, looking at that door—now that going through it was at least a viable possibility—the difficulty of making this decision occupied almost every waking thought. The gravity of what we were contemplating was huge. Moving forward in this direction would remove all second-guessing as an option.

Was this the answer? Should we wait for another? Or as my heart was known to ask in some of my more worrisome moments: Should we rethink this whole missionary thing altogether?

But sometimes, when tangled in a knot of indecision, part of what we need is not more prayer but a better memory. Part of looking ahead involves looking back.

Do you remember the scene from Joshua 4, where the people of Israel had crossed the dried-up Jordan River on foot and planted their first steps on Canaan soil? After they were safely across, God instructed a handful of men to go back and choose twelve big stones from the middle of the exposed riverbed (while they still had the chance), lift them up on their shoulders, and carry them into the camp. Joshua took those stones—one to represent each tribe of Israel—and stacked them up in the center of the meeting grounds. The purpose of these stones, God said, was to be a sign, a memorial of what He had done that day by parting the swollen Jordan River so they could walk into the Promised Land. As impossible as it had looked before, look where they were now! Look what God had accomplished, right out where they could see it.

The reason I mention this Old Testament moment is because of what I think too often happens when you and

I stand at the significant doorways of life today—whether they're locked tight and needing a good shove, or whether they're partway open but still obscuring the view around the next corner. We tend to sorta hang up there. To hesitate. Feeling the need to move ahead but not the courage to do it, we start looking around for anything we can grab onto, something solid to give us some confident backup support for this bold maneuver we're about to make. And when we do look back, what do we see?

Is a stack of stones there? A pile of memorial moments? Reminders of times when God came through during a real faith crisis and proved just how capable He is of seeing us through to the next doorway?

Or is it blank? Just a bare floor. No recorded history. No crossroads of life when, after stepping up to a line where either God was going to have to come through for us in a big way or we were going to fall flat on our face, we punched the faith pedal anyway. And got a new stone for our stack.

Courtney and I—like you, I'm sure—can look back in our marriage, in our kids' lives, in our extended family's lives, and rake up some pretty good-sized rocks if we're looking for them, rocks that match the size of what God over time has done to heal things, correct things, save things, redeem things. Especially in those months following my experience with God in the barn, when we intentionally made some decisions we honestly didn't feel like we could pull off—quit the business? sell the stock? pay for the adoption? put the house on the market?—we grabbed hold, sucked in our breath, and jumped off with nobody but God to catch us. And what do you know— sitting there on the ledge where we landed, a ledge we couldn't even see when we'd made our leap for it—was another big stone. Another marker for God's memory pile.

Those stones don't just form a stack; they build confidence. They tell us, the next time we're up against a doorway, feeling Him calling us from the other side, we can wipe the sweat out of our eyes, look around, catch a glimpse of those stones in our peripheral vision, and remember—"Oh yeah, we've been here before. And look what He did with worries that seemed every bit as big at the time as the ones we're facing right now."

Those stones tell a story.

They help us remember.

And when we use them to hurl our faith through new doors of challenge and God-inspired opportunity, they become part of making all-new memories of confidence that'll stack up behind us when we need them again.

And that, my friend, is when a lot of Christian people stop finding you so radically weird and start finding your faith really contagious. Your confidence inspires their confidence. Your joy makes them hungry for their own joy as well. Your fire makes them want to go start a new fire themselves.

Our little Sunday school class back in Brentwood, Tennessee, is one clear example of this. Financially, they've helped in large part to put us (and keep us) on the mission field—which is no small undertaking. Another family from that class has actually picked up and moved here also, five doors down from us, serving the Lord and happier than they've ever been. But even the ones who are still back home in America are *on mission*, I'm telling you—forty couples mobilized to go do crazy stuff for Jesus in our community and through their various relationships.

We see the class e-mails when they're sent out and—man!—Courtney and I sit over here in South Africa, eight hours ahead of everybody, and go, "Wow, what's happening with those people back there?" They amaze *me* with what they're doing—and I'm supposed to be the missionary here, the one with all the snake and spider stories to come back and tell. But, no, that's not the way it is. As God motivates them and they respond in obedience, they are incrementally changing the climate and temperature of an eight-to-ten-thousand member church by giving sacrificially, serving with abandon, going hard after what really matters, and basically just living out the gospel through their marriages and families and together as a body of believers.

Me—shoot, I was so hard for God to deal with, He had to send me clear across the world to get me to understand what surrender was all about. He must have known I was *never* going to get off that hamster wheel as long as I was out on the farm watching TV commercials and deciding I needed whatever they were selling. My friends who are still there—a lot of them are getting the message of surrender without pulling their kids out of school or walking off their jobs like I did. But they're missionaries just the same—in their homes and in their neighbor-hoods, up the road and in the city.

And every time they barrel through another door, as God keeps calling them on, the stack of stones that's starting to pile up around our little community of faith is getting huge and impossible not to see.

Isn't that what you want? To be watching that stack grow deeper and fuller behind you, where you quit being afraid to do *anything* if you sense God is leading you there—especially not because you're afraid of what some-body else will think. When you're free from worrying about that, when you're just swiveling toward whichever opening God wants you stepping through next—from the small, everyday, on-the-way kind of stuff to the much more permanent commitments of your time and your future—that's when you're in the sweetest spot on earth, no matter where you lay your head at night. You're walking within your calling. You're living in surrendered obedience at every moment. And as much as you need to be doing it yourself, the people around you need to be seeing it.

Even the Christian people.

I feel more invigorated today in Africa than ever before in all my life. By a country mile. What I see over here on a daily basis, what I see in the people who con-stantly impact our lives (while we're officially supposed to be over here changing theirs) is beyond my wildest hopes for what I always wanted in a job, what I always wanted for my family, and what I always wanted for myself. God has opened a lot of amazing doors for us on this side of surrender, but He's sometimes done it by making us walk through some tightly locked doors to get there.

"A crucible for silver, and a smelter for gold," the Bible says, but "the LORD is the tester of hearts" (Prov. 17:3). Does He open doors for us? Sure. But what He really wants is our hearts, so that He can lead us wherever He wants us, whenever He wants to do it, and lead us deeper into His presence and blessing at the same time.

Our world, not to mention your friends and your church, needs to see that kind of faith and passion in somebody. Not the kind that just blends in, splashing around in the shallow end. Haven't we all had enough of that mess? I'm talking about the kind that launches off the high dive, inspiring other people who are sitting around to say, "Hey, if he can do that, surely I can do it too."

And yes, we can—because the only thing crazier than a Christian who's radically following Christ are the ones who let certain Christians get in their heads and stunt their surrender.

Which one of those crazy people do you want to be?

Chapter 5

The Family That Surrenders Together

B ut what about your kids?
That's the number-one thing people ask me: "How are your kids doing?"

And they're not always asking as if they really want to find out, but more like they think they already know the answer. They'll usually look at me sort of sideways, shaking their head a little, their eyes squinting up, pretty sure the truth is much more unpleasant than I'm probably willing to admit or recognize. "Those poor, poor children," they seem to be saying. "What chance do they have at a normal life? What are they going to do for an education? What if they get sick and need better health care than you can find for them over there in Africa? What's likely to become of their future? Think of all the opportunities they're missing out on."

Code word for: "I'd sure never do that to *my* children!"

But, you know, those people don't really concern me very much. After all, it's not *their* children they're talking about. It's *mine*. And I guarantee you, there's not a single question they could ask or a single opinion they could hold that I haven't already thought about at least a thousand times before—in hi-def color and personal detail.

So as a general rule, I give people like that the short-form answer. *We're fine, thanks. How are you?* They wouldn't believe anything I told them anyway. No, the people who draw out the longest discussions from me are the ones who aren't asking just because they're skeptically curious about how we're all getting along. The people who really tug at my heart are the ones who ask because they themselves have a sense that God may be calling them to a whole new level of surrender and sacrifice. And that means the kids they're asking about are not really ours, but their own. What might happen to *their* kids (that's what they actually want to know) if their family were to do something so drastically different in their lifestyle?

As much as a mom or dad may wish for a deeper sense of mission and purpose for themselves, they're likely to stop short of doing much about it if they're afraid it might rankle their children too much. As frustrated as a parent may feel about the round-and-round futility of their lives, is it ever worth trying to goose it off-center at the risk of upsetting the kids' equilibrium? Is it fair to make them deal with the necessary fallout—to make them put up with maybe having less, with being different, with experiencing change, with not being able to go over and spend the night at Grandma's on a whim? You've got to think about the kids first, right?

Well . . . right.

But maybe that's exactly what you're doing when you follow up on the nudge God is giving you in your spirit, the one that says there's more to this life than what you're settling for—more freedom of movement, more ongoing fulfillment, more of that feeling of being smack in the middle of what pleases the heart of God and what truly matters in people's lives.

Maybe nothing could be better for your kids than that.

Did you ever think of it that way?

Listen, I know all about that little inner dialogue you may be having in your head right now. I'll bet I could guess every question you're asking. And honestly, something's probably wrong with you if you're not asking them. The thought of being seriously and fully available to God is not some overnight lark. It's not just a "Hey, let's drive up to the mountains this weekend," and then leaving so quickly that you don't really have time to think too hard about what you're tossing in the suitcase. No, this is a big deal. It's walk-the-floor kind of praying. This stuff means business.

So, yeah, I wondered those same things (a lot!) during those tentative weeks and months when I was first grappling with everything, trying to think through what this very definite calling from God really meant for us—for *all* of us—especially as it started picking up steam, when it started to sound like it wasn't going to end with an altar call and a heartfelt confession and my two-millionth promise to be a better Christian. No, this was way different. It wasn't just one of those occasional spikes in my spiritual testosterone, where I'd straighten up for a few weeks, read my Bible more, try to actually pay attention to God instead of ignoring Him half the time. I was fully aware that He was unsettling me for a reason, and I couldn't get away from it. Things were changing. This was all-new territory through here, the kind that called for a much more comprehensive game plan. And from where I stood, I couldn't see it stopping before it turned the whole house upside down—Courtney, kids, and all.

So I don't know how many nights I stared up into the soft darkness of the ceiling over our bed, wide awake, feeling all my frets and worries pacing around in nervous circles inside my head. God had been telling me to surrender, to trust Him, to put my life and future completely in His hands. But I wasn't so sure He had noticed something very important: my life and future had picked up a wife and several young children along the way. So whatever this *surrender* deal involved couldn't help but also involve a lot of other special people to me as well.

And I didn't know if I could do that.

Couldn't I just commit to doing something myself? Something that would only take a chunk out of my *own* time, not everybody else's? Something that would only cost *me*? Something that wouldn't disrupt the lives of my whole family, except for maybe having to do without me for a few weeks or weekends out of the year?

But here's what I didn't understand for a long time: this *surrender* that God demands of us is not merely a price to pay. More important (and boy, more than I ever realized before), it is an on-ramp to the abundant Christian life. Unreal. Better than ever. And that meant if I was to shield my family from shelling out the sacrifice with me—based on a normal, parental desire to protect and provide for them—I would also be shortchanging them from the boatload of blessings that would flow back into their lives as a result. Not just mine, theirs too.

That's no pie-in-the-sky talk. That's just the truth.

What, then, are we really saying when we think, "Lord, you know I can't speak for everybody else in this house. How can you expect me to do what You're telling me to do when I'm not the only one affected by this?" But if you'll keep pressing into that statement—that question—working out what it means and what it reveals about the condition of your heart, you may find the same thought starting to morph into this one: "How can I stand before God knowing I *cheated* everybody else in the house from experiencing the fruit of my obedience to Him?"

I speak for myself and my whole family when I say: "What are you waiting for?"

All or Nothing

Some of our best church friends, Tate and Brooke Elder, were part of a group that came to visit us over here in Cape Town a few years ago. And like what happens to many of us, that kind of temporary getaway from the rutted routine, going out to see the world from another vantage point, was an enormous head-clearing experience for them. I don't care who you are, I don't care where you go, the opportunity to see human need and the reality of God's mercy in a context so very foreign to your own is a good way to rearrange your wiring.

For some—for most—it's a true memory-maker that sends them back home with a zeal for looking at life in a whole new way. It changes them. Changes their perspective. Changes the way their food tastes, changes the way the stores look, changes the way they worship and give and parent and operate. But for others—like Tate—God on occasion has been known to say, even while a person is still on the ground in a missions setting, "This is where I want you, son. Right here. And I'm telling you, you won't be happy till you get here."

In the early weeks of their return to the States, that's exactly what was on his heart. Those feelings that usually filter back into Monday morning meetings and Tuesday night leftovers were still churning in his gut. Those resolutions that typically begin to stair-step down from active compassion to something only slightly north of distant pity—they weren't going downhill for him at all. Something wasn't right about the old normal any longer. God had given him a vision for something more. And it wasn't letting up. If anything, it was getting stronger.

What did that mean?

What was God wanting?

He and Brooke, naturally, found lots of offhand moments after coming home when the topic of typical conversation would transport them back to their African trip—what they'd seen, what they'd felt, how its impact had touched both of them at very deep, spiritual levels. But there came a point, observing his tone of voice at times, when she realized he was sounding kind of serious about this thing, like he actually might be giving some lengthy thought to "Honey, what if we . . ."

"No. Stop right there."

"Brooke, I know, I'm just trying to be honest with you about what I'm feeling. It's like, ever since we've been back, the mission field just seems to be calling my name."

"No. It doesn't."

"Okay."

"No. It's not."

"Okay, okay."

"Tate, we've got two girls to raise and protect. We've got a life to consider here. Yes, I know what Courtney and Joey are doing over there is wonderful. It sneaks into your heart when you see it. It feels so good, and they tell it so well. But it's not for us, dear. You and I can't be trotting off doing that." That's all there was to it.

End of discussion.

But I want you to picture Brooke for a moment, sitting here with us at our African dinner table—after having been here as a new missionary family themselves for about three months with daughters Abby and Olivia—telling me what had happened to bring about this whole change of mind in her.

She had gone for a mid-morning swim at their neighborhood YMCA. Very ordinary. Normal workout routine. After finishing her laps, she had pulled herself out of the pool, was just sitting there on the edge, catching her breath, getting ready to go towel off and go on with the rest of her day, when this thought came floating through her mind, as though out of nowhere—*I'll let you make this decision, you know. I'll leave it up to you.*

It was like, for a moment, the pool disappeared. The echo of splashing water disappeared. Her awareness of other people being around her disappeared. And the pace of her heartbeat, which had been slowing down toward a resting rate, began ticking faster again, climbing back in the direction of full exertion speed.

She knew immediately what that feeling meant . . . and what that *thought* had meant.

Brooke knew God well enough to know His voice when she heard it. And what He was saying was that He was more than willing to let her say no to what her husband was sensing (and trying hard now not to express to her) about a possible future in missions. They never needed to speak of it again. It was a closed issue, if that's the way she wanted it. She could go on about her life as if no other parts of the world hardly existed beyond the radius of her normal, suburban driving loop and the Florida beach every summer.

Off you go.

Have fun.

But with the panting rhythm of her breath the only sound she could hear, her heart suddenly began coming completely undone, puddling up around her on the pool deck, along with the water still dripping from her wet hair. "It broke me. I just sat there and wept. The lifeguards were coming up and asking, 'Is everything okay? Are you all right?' I mean, I was having that kind of moment, where everybody around me could see it, right out there in public. And all I could think was—we're going. *How can I be saying this? How can I be considering this? I can't believe I'm even thinking this, but—oh, Lord, we're going, aren't we . . .*"

Later that afternoon, when Tate walked in the door from work, Brooke caught him before he could even put his stuff down. "I need to tell you something that happened to me today," she said, "but before I do, I just want you to know . . .

"You're right—we need to go."

Absolutely true story.

And the reason I tell you this is because, for all the Tate Elders out there, for all the people who can tell in their heart that God is clearly busting up their appetite for business-as-usual, He knows you cannot do this alone. He didn't call you to surrender—He *isn't* calling you to surrender—expecting you to abandon your wife and kids on the back steps of your obedience.

He knows you're married (if you are).

He knows you have kids (if you do).

He knows you're connected to your family at both the heart and the hip. As you *should* be.

And if He's calling you, then He's calling them too—not right away maybe, not without a lot of prayer and patience in between. But part of your surrender and putting your full trust in God means trusting that He's working inside every one of your family relationships to line this puppy up in the direction He's intending it to go.

As my dad said to me, very early in this spiritual journey of ours, "If God has told you something as the man of the house, you won't need to sell your wife on it, because He knows the importance of that relationship. If you pray for her, He's bringing her on."

If that's where this page of the book is finding you today—desiring God like never before, but half afraid to even mention it to your spouse or to dare going there in your thinking, in terms of your children and the possible ramifications—it's time for your prayer life to start becoming as regular and automatic as your breathing life.

Pray.

Pray together.

Pray when you're apart.

Pray in places you've never prayed before.

I used to be scared to death to pray in front of Courtney. You know why? I didn't want her to hear how lame and clunky and shallow my prayers really were. I was so self-conscious about it. I was embarrassed. It was awkward. Just felt weird and artificial somehow.

But beginning with those days when God grabbed such a tight hold on me, I knew I needed to get over my silly hesitation. God does amazing things sometimes when we do just some of the simplest things—things we've always known we should do, things it doesn't take a seminary genius to figure out, things that honestly should never have been a question in the first place if we hadn't gotten so busy and distracted and self-assured to think we didn't really need them anymore.

So start there. Just hold hands and pray. As a couple. Get your Bible out and read it. Soak it in. Take it slow. Let Him speak. Write it out. Journal whatever comes to mind as you hear Him come alive to you through His Word. Lay it all out there before Him without an agenda or any attempt to manipulate anybody. Just put the full weight and pressure of all that stuff on God.

He's the one who started this. And so He's the one on the hook for keeping it going. Your job is just to surrender, to trust, to believe, to follow. His job is to speak where your spouse can hear Him, while He keeps filling you up with the spiritual strength you need each day to remain steadfast, waiting for Him to show you what's next, and next, and next, and then next.

I'm not saying that if you think God is calling you to a particular form of mission, you're automatically right for charging ahead and she's automatically wrong for putting on the brakes. That's above my pay grade to figure out. I'm just saying that God can be trusted to lead you. Together. At His pace and in His timing. And as long as you're beating a steady path toward surrender, you can be sure you're heading in the right direction, moving toward the place where His specific plans for your life can meet up with you.

With both of you.

With all of you.

Wherever God takes you, He's taking you together.

Marriage Portrait

I don't know what your marriage is like today. Only you know that.

But I know what most marriages are like, for most people. They're strained. They're stressful. They're tired, stretched thin, overworked. They do have their brighter moments, for sure, but most moments stay pretty much confined to surface-level and Saturday errands. A lot of their time is spent with all eyes on the television or in separate rooms on their techno-devices. They're interrupted by schedules that conflict with one another's at almost every turn. Their spiritual growth is largely relegated to Sundays, meaning most days go by with little more than a canned blessing over the supper plates and a quick good-night over the kids when they're tucked into bed. Consistency is erratic. Blame goes around.

They're worried about a dozen things that can never be fixed by worry, and yet they're not worried enough about things that could probably afford the attention. They're slowly growing bitter and disillusioned with each other, many of them inching closer all the time to becoming another failed marriage statistic for the census takers. Their pictures look all smiley and chummy on Facebook—parties and picnics and goofy poses with their birthday presents—but underneath there's often a lot of bickering, old wounds, fresh offenses, and unmet needs. It's not always as pretty a picture as it seems. They hurt as often as they're happy. Sometimes more.

Does that about cover it?

I realize there's a chance I'm overgeneralizing or being way too pessimistic here, maybe painting it a little worse than it is. But probably not by much. We cover up the dirt pretty well. People don't know.

But *we* know.

We know our status quo.

And while hopefully your marriage is one of those exceptions that generally breaks the rule, I just wonder why most people—Christian people—feel so certain that surrendering themselves fully to God as a couple is just asking too much of them and their situation, that it's sure to mess everything up. Mess *what* up?

Their snippy in-law relationships?

Their crazy calendars?

Their insensitive attitudes?

Their backlog of dysfunctions?

Their lazy disciplines and habits?

Their subtle games and deceptions?

Long memories they won't forgive?

What?

Courtney and I—I'll just tell you, we weren't hitting on all cylinders as a couple, even during the run-up period to what eventually became our radical change of course and life plan. Nobody would've thought it—same as nobody would think it of you, I'll bet—but the distance was slowly growing. The pace of life was keeping us consistently strung out and short-fused. I had a hard time saying no to people or passing up opportunities to do the things I wanted to do—at least not without copping an attitude if I didn't get my way. Love was there, of course, but it was getting harder to feel and easier to misinterpret. Did we have a good marriage? Yeah, I mean, we had young kids at home. It's kind of hard not to get caught up in the fun and excitement of that. But could it have been better? My, yes. A lot better. At least I know I sure could've been a whole lot better at my part.

But I pause here because—I'm truly at a loss to know how to describe what God has done within our relationship by taking us on this journey together.

Arguing just doesn't happen in our house anymore.

She doesn't complain. I don't bristle up at her.

There's rarely miscommunication between us.

No secrets. No motives. No chilly receptions.

Don't get the wrong idea, now—we're both individually a long way from perfect. But the love and trust and unity we experience on a daily basis as a couple is like nothing I've ever felt before. I didn't know this kind of marriage really existed—at least not after black-and-white television went off the air.

When I pray with Courtney now, she is hanging on for dear life, because there's an honest confidence and boldness in my relationship with God that just wasn't there before. And when *she* prays—my goodness—the deep faith and compassion and strength she bundles together, the genuine willingness she feels to follow God into whatever situation He chooses to send us, the love she has for people, for our kids, for me . . .

It's not normal, really, the marriage we have now—or at least it's nowhere close to what it was. It's unbelievable. God has put me on the mission field, side by side with my very best friend in the world. That is no cliché or overstatement, no joke. At any moment of the day, there's nobody I'd rather be with. Nobody. And as I watch her keep growing spiritually, as the Lord increasingly becomes her truest source of affirmation and supply, she pushes me to want more of Him too. She frees me up as a man to go out exploring His will for my life every day as a Christ-centered business leader, mentor, and friend. She makes me more eager and enthusiastic than ever to become the right kind of husband and father that she and our children need, because I know without a doubt she's pulling for me and wants me to succeed. And my devotion and trust in her keeps her from worrying one second that I'll disapprove of how she spends her time or where she places her priorities.

When I'm low and struggling, she's there to pull me up. And when *she's* feeling particularly beat down and fatigued—missing home and family and all the familiar things she so graciously does without—God helps me be the one who pulls the trailer for a little while, until He's stoked her fire back up again for the next leg of the trip.

It's beautiful.

And I know for a fact this just was not going to happen—ever!—before *surrender* became our rallying cry. I feel pretty sure we'd have eventually become, if not litigants in divorce court, at least an old pair of in-home enemies who'd roll our eyes and mutter under our breath and never really intend to like each other anymore.

And to think—I could have chosen *that*? Over *this*? Over the marriage I've got now? Whenever I wasn't too sure about surrendering, I was trying to hang onto *that*?

When you and I finally trust God with full control of our lives, one of the blessings waiting up His sleeve for us is the gift of a renewed marriage. Surrender doesn't mess it up; surrender turns it completely around. At least that's been our experience.

And the same goes for the kids . . .

Do It for the Children

"How are the kids?" You mean the ones without the education and the opportunities? The ones missing out on all the advantages we snatched them away from by whisking them off to the Dark Ages—I mean, the Dark Continent? I'm not meaning to turn this into a Christmas letter, but . . . just to give you an idea . . .

Briley, our oldest—twelve years old—basically has her own ministry here in South Africa. She speaks two and a half languages now: English, Afrikaans, and a good bit of Xhosa (pronounced CO-sa)—one of those "click" languages. Very cool thing to hear. And she uses these skills she's developing (mixed with that Southern drawl of hers, which she came by very honestly) to connect with the people around her and to make new friends—to help and serve and do anything possible to comfort and care for others. Yes, she's seen poverty and death and disease—things we're conditioned as Americans to try shielding from our kids' view. It's forced us to have certain conversations with her, earlier than we ordinarily would. But I can take Briley into any home in the area, from the wealthiest to the most destitute, and she can interact with anybody there at a level of maturity and charm that just amazes me.

She's fine. She's great.

Braxton, our much quieter ten-year-old—you can see him truly coming into his own personality over here, secure in himself and succeeding in every arena, fully engaged in life and very much into what our family's doing here. The past two years, at the end of school, both he and Briley have been given the "Emotional Achievement Award," which—yeah, first time I heard it, I had the same reaction as you. Sounded like the everybody-gets-a-trophy deal, the good sportsmanship prize. But people were coming up to us afterward as if they'd won the presidential medal or something. It's actually based on a whole profile of different factors—good grades being part of it, of course, but also other ingredients that go into the holistic makeup of a child. It's the top award in school. And of the five that were handed out—across every grade level—our kids got two of them. Never happened before, they told us, where two siblings had won.

So Braxton's fine. He's doing great.

Barron's our little six-year-old spark plug, a nine-volt-battery kind of kid who—all he wants to do is wrestle and mix it up and get as gross and dirty as a little boy can get. We'll drive down into Masi, a terribly poor township near our home, and you'll often hear the little African boys calling toward us from the side of the road, "Bar-RON!" They love that little firecracker spirit in him. And after we've been back in America on our summer furlough every year—six weeks of reconnecting with friends and family and big piles of Mexican food—he's one of the first of the kids, about a month deep into all this attention and recreation, to say, "Dad, when are we going home? I'm ready to go back."

There's sure nothing wrong with that kid.

Bristol, you met her in the last chapter. And our newest one, Baylor, just recently born here in South Africa, has given us a whole other chapter to write, a living testimony to the ongoing faithfulness of God's provision and the blessings of surrender on our family.

They're fine. My kids are fine.

No, they don't always get along. They pick at each other and get crossways over the littlest stuff sometimes.

They're no different than anybody else's children. But they're growing wise at a young age, both wide and deep, and embracing experiences that will impact them for the rest of their lives. And they're getting to live it all out with a mom and dad who—while messing it up bad on a lot of days—are obviously risking everything to be as obedient to the call of God as we can humanly be. And so the stack of stones piling up behind Courtney and me—the many reminders of God's protection and grace and deliverance—are being scooted up into our children's lives as well, where they can add to it themselves and build it up even higher with their own stones, the ones He gives them nearly every day.

So I don't think I'm depleting my kids by having them over here; I'm watching God grow them into Christ-loving, Bible-reading, prayer-dependent warriors in training for the next generation of kingdom conquest.

And it is an awesome thing to watch.

Back when I was living the half-empty life—the one I tried to fill up with all the horses and horsepower—I was actually zapping my kids' energy and potential by trying to buy their way into fun and fulfillment. I see it now. Without ever meaning to, I was setting them up to fail. I was allowing the world's way of thinking and navigating to impinge on everything we did. By being too afraid to trust God and to line up my family with His biblical way of doing things, I was actually undermining everybody— from Courtney all the way down. I was holding them hostage to my limited view of life and success, not realizing

FULFILLED

that God is totally serious when He tells us to seek first His kingdom and His righteousness, "and all these things will be provided for you" (Matt. 6:33).

"All these things."

They're all landing right under my own rooftop now.

We're experiencing things today as a family that would've never been possible if I hadn't fully surrendered my life to Christ as the spiritual head of our home and started leading them as a man who was passionately in love with God enough until it bled through. That's not bragging on me; that's bragging on Him. That's just agreeing with the way His Word draws it up.

Why in the world should we expect our kids to be sold out to God if their *dad's* not sold out to God, if they're not seeing obedience, faith, and surrender practiced in their own living room? How is my wife supposed to stay filled up spiritually and emotionally if I'm draining her all the time by my lack of vision, love, and leadership? There's no synergy, no ministry, no life, no nothing. If anybody's going forward, they're having to fight me or go around me to do it. Nobody's experiencing any abundant life that way.

I guess, really, whenever we back away from surrender because we doubt that God can extend His protection over our children's lives as well as our own, we're actually revealing that God is not on the throne of our hearts after all. Know who is? *Our kids are.* I'm not meaning to sound negligent here because, yes, God has given us responsibility and stewardship over our children. We have a clear role to play according to the biblical pattern as parents. But if I'm letting them keep me from following God's call, then who am I really serving here? God or them?

And if that sounds harsh and unfeeling, just know that what I really mean is what I've seen with my own eyes. A man's total surrender to God as the spiritual leader of his family creates the ideal situation for every one of his children to live in and be nurtured. Whatever you're afraid your kids will lose and give up by following their crazy dad or mom into absolute trust and confident obedience, you can kiss those worries good-bye.

"God, You do know I've got a family, don't You?"

Yeah, He knows.

You don't mind if He just wants to bless the socks off of them, do you?

Safe Travels

A month or two after our meeting with John Thomas, where he first introduced us to the ministry of Living Hope and the opportunities beginning to develop through their job creation program, I woke up next to Courtney at our family's vacation home up in the Blue Ridge Mountains. I'm not sure what had turned the dial for me that morning, lying there in the quiet, praying as I slowly emerged from the night's sleep. But I rolled over to Courtney—woke her up, actually, without really meaning to—and simply said, as matter-of-fact as this: "I think God's calling us to Cape Town."

She spun slowly around toward me, smiled a sweet, warm, contented smile, and just quietly said, "I've been there for two weeks, babe. I was just waiting for *you* to come."

Talk about a stone-stacking moment in my personal journey. Here I was, the one who'd started all this lofty talk about surrender and release and missions and everything. And in as little as six months' time, having led out pretty boldly (I thought) as husband and father, taking some drastic steps toward being completely faith-based with my family—Mr. Spiritual Giant in the making— here was my wife waiting on *me* to catch up.

How 'bout that?

So there wasn't any doubt what to do next. Not anymore.

I got up, rang Scott Harris on his phone in Tennessee. And before the sun had barely risen across the tree-lined mountain peaks in *South Carolina*, we had raised anchor as a couple and family for our new home in *South Africa*.

"I don't know what this really means, Scott," I told him, "but we're in. Whatever the process, you're free to start cranking it up today. We're going."

And so began about a year-long endeavor of getting ourselves ready, getting Bristol's adoption situated, getting some good training under our belt, getting our spiritual and physical house in order. By this time the next summer, I was preparing to fly out for South Africa, solo trip—like a cowboy going out ahead of my family, staking my claim, scouting the trail alone before hitching my wife and kids into the wagon and blazing out on our bold, new pioneering adventure.

But the Tuesday night before I was to head out the following Monday . . .

Tragedy struck.

The phone rang—it was my Aunt Sonya—my mom's much younger little sister, who's actually more like my cousin because we're so close in age. She and her husband, Drason, were at the hospital with Bane, their nine-month-old son, completely in shock and begging for prayer. Knowing we needed to do something fast, Courtney tore off for Nashville while I stayed home with the kids.

What could possibly be going wrong with Bane? He was a perfectly healthy, perfectly developing little baby. In fact, he and his family had been over at the house just a few days before, over the weekend. I'd held him and made faces at him, giggled with him. Everything was great.

But he had awakened on Tuesday morning with a temperature. Kind of high—high enough that Sonya thought she'd call and ask if they could work him in at the doctor's office later in the day. She took him in around noon, the doctor examined him good, said he appeared okay, just to take him home and keep him resting, call back if his fever keeps climbing.

It did.

And by that evening, my tiny baby cousin, Bane Beasley, was hemorrhaging from meningitis on a table in Vanderbilt Children's Hospital.

Soon I got word from Courtney . . .

He was dead.

Sitting home that night, getting that call from my wife—"No, no, no," I said, "that just can't be." But it was. And it shook me. This wasn't the send-off I was hoping to get. As if I wasn't edgy and nervous enough about picking up my kids and moving them clear around the world into the total unknown, now this? Really? Right as I'm fixin' to head out and make this official?

On Saturday, two days before my flight, I was dressed up as a pallbearer, sitting through probably the most unexpected funeral service I'd ever attended. And later, when the families were together and I found a moment to visit with Sonya alone, she was almost the one trying to comfort me instead of the other way around. "I'm so sorry, Joey," she said. "I know this is really complicating things for your family and your trip."

But God, in His own personal way, had spent some time through the week helping me synthesize these two drastic experiences—theirs and ours. And while my heart broke for her and Drason and everyone else affected so closely by this stunning event, I said to her, "Sonya," grabbing hold of both hands to be sure I had her attention, "let me tell you what I've learned from Bane's death—and I hope at some point this will bring some comfort to you. You told me he went from being completely healthy to being in heaven within one day—right here within fifteen minutes of the finest children's hospital in the country, probably in the world. You know what that means? It means I can't keep my kids alive here, any more than I can kill 'em by moving them away to Africa." I got on that plane Monday morning with more release and conviction than I'd ever felt before, because I knew—I *knew!*—my life and my families' lives were not at all in my hands, but totally and completely in God's.

You and I can try pocketing ourselves and our kids inside the most ideal living conditions on the planet. We can wrap them up and keep out the cold and think we're doing everything possible to ward off trouble. But no gated community or health-care access or street-lit sidewalks or any so-called precaution is secure enough to keep our families from experiencing whatever can happen, anywhere they are, at any moment of the day, no matter how safe it may feel or how protected they may seem. When we give up our children to the loving care of God, we're only choosing to agree with Him on what's already taking place anyway: His absolute sovereignty over everything that touches us and the people we care about.

What they need from us most is not the house we live in or the good school district or the neighborhood playground or any of those surface things that make us feel like they're so much better off here than anywhere else. They can shrivel up spiritually or run off with a Harley rider just as easily from a nice corner lot on a comfy street as from any other location in the world. But they are always in the best place they can be if they've got a mom and dad in deep relationship with God, prayerfully following His lead, loving each other, and inviting their kids into the family's journey of faith.

So instead of fighting it, why not just go ahead and live in it? In surrender. In confidence. In daring to trust that His best interests for your marriage and your children are far more appealing than whatever you'd been hoping to accomplish with your own puny little plans.

If you're waiting to let go spiritually because it feels like you're letting go of your role in the family, or because you feel like your spouse would never go for it, why don't you just sit back and let God take care of that part? What's impossible to us is a piece of cake to Him.

He might even serve you up a big slice of nice surprises to go along with your side order of surrender—things you never saw coming, things you've always wished for, but could never seem to bring about, no matter how hard you worked or how intentionally you tried.

In fact, based on what I've seen so far in our own lives, I think I can pretty much guarantee it.

The best days in your family's life are just waiting on your surrender.

Chapter 6

Tunnel Vision

Six months in South Africa.

On bold, Billy Graham mission with God.

And basically, I'd become a cucumber salesman.

I guess I just thought—oh, I don't know what I'd thought. You do nothing else but plan out and pray through this move for a year, you feel the tingle of doing something wildly unconventional, you bust loose from the corporate culture, you work your kids up into a lather of excitement. And after all the back-slapping, crate-packing, prayer-intensive work it takes to leave, you're over here experiencing the kind of "firsts" you never expected to happen in your lifetime—sitting on your own back patio in a foreign country, eating ostrich and warthog off the grill, meeting people every day who grew up in places you'd only seen on a world map in your fifth-grade classroom.

In some ways, I suppose, it's like taking any new job. They court you hard for two or three months, treating you like somebody special, fly you in for a second interview and a handshake with the company president, first-name basis all around the boardroom, everybody acting like they've been waiting all week to meet you. Then you're hired. And the work starts. But after a few months, the "new guy" label starts to wear thin, and you're just another shirt on another Monday afternoon in another staff meeting, half wishing you'd stayed behind at the place you'd been before.

Don't think being a Christian missionary somehow sanctifies all these feelings.

And so somewhere between March and April, the year following our arrival in Cape Town, I was already asking some of the same questions I'd been asking from my deck in College Grove: "Is this it? Is this really what I'm supposed to be doing with my life?"

For seven days, we'd been distributing our first crop of cucumbers to local markets—my first initiative in job creation and entrepreneurism—thirteen hundred high-quality units of product, each a foot long or more, handpicked and packaged to retail specs, then driven across town in the back of our pickup. It was hard, time-consuming work, making sure we were providing our new vendor partners exactly what they wanted . . . when and where they wanted it. We didn't yet know how our stuff would sell, whether we'd satisfy both retailer and end-consumer, or what the long-term outcome of our plans and ideas would prove to be. And as I was hauling another load into the family grocer that was nearest to our campus, I did my best to put on a good face—the health-care executive turned delivery boy.

Rodgers Fruit Stand is run by a family who welcomed our stock of vegetables from the very beginning and were glad to promote them as a Living Way product, indirectly supporting our ministry. Super-friendly people. Mrs. Rodgers was manning the checkout line when I walked in that day, but she glanced over and said hello.

"How are our cucumbers doing?" I asked.

You won't believe what she said—or at least the way she said it.

"Joey, I was just telling the customers that our Christian friends are really being blessed by their Jesus."

"Ma'am?"

"Because your cucumbers are just flying off the shelf."

What? I heaved my bundle of fresh goods toward the back of the store, nudging the curtain with my shoulder that led into their warehouse area, hearing her words still rattling around in my dazed skull: "our Christian friends . . . being blessed by their Jesus." After setting down the box, I reached over and grabbed an empty milk crate, flipped it around on its bottom, and sat my full weight on it—not to catch my breath, but just to be sure I'd fully absorbed what I'd just heard.

Cucumbers.

God was drawing glory to His name through cucumbers.

And even, He seemed to say, *through a certain cucumber salesman I could name.*

This journey from dissatisfaction to surrender—in our case, from America to South Africa—has been and continues to be a steady breakdown of pride, a redefinition of success, a new awareness of His involvement in every single aspect of our lives, and a steady piling-up of reasons why my best option is always just to trust Him, sight unseen, even though He's under no obligation to tell me what He's doing unless He decides I need to know.

Whatever limitations I'd grown accustomed to placing on Him, He shows me almost every day that my view of Him is too small. And whatever demands I'd always felt entitled to make on the importance and parameters of my personal role in His kingdom, He shows me that my view of myself is too big.

And the patient process He employs in correcting these misconceptions—if we're really serious about surrender—goes a long way toward clearing up our poor spiritual eyesight and helping us enjoy the settled freedom of just being His servant.

It's a surefire cure for tunnel vision.

Let's Make a Deal

On my first trip to South Africa the previous August, John Thomas had walked me around the Living Hope campus, introduced me to all kinds of people, and showed me some of the things they'd been developing through their local empowerment program in its first three or four years of existence.

And the whole time, I'm thinking, "Okay, but what am *I* going to be doing here?"

The weight of knowing my wife and kids were sitting back home, counting down the number of sleeps left before making their tearful good-byes, was always hanging there in the back of my mind. Even with all these new sights to see and the large amount of information to absorb, the main thing I was feeling was responsibility for what my family was about to experience. I wanted to make the best use of these seven days, arrange a place for us to live, see where the kids would be going to school, meet their teachers, stuff like that. But at the same time, I felt pressure on myself to come back with some fairly concrete ideas for what my work would entail and how secure (relatively speaking) this whole job creation setup appeared to be. So far, it was still a little murky in my mind.

But John, during a lull in our meeting, perhaps suspecting I was feeling a little antsy for more specifics, said, "I've noticed some tunnels down the road for sale. That might be something we can look at."

"Tunnels? You mean, like—underground tunnels?"

"No, no—what do you call them, uh . . . greenhouses."

"Oh, okay, I gotcha."

"Would you like to go look at them?"

So we headed out toward his little red car that was parked on the street. I approached it from the wrong side of the road, tried to get in on the wrong side of the car (South Africans drive in the left lane, driver's seat on the right). *Nice going, Grace.* But after a little nervous embarrassment, I was off with John to see these so-called "tunnels," located about four miles away.

Turned out, a Zimbabwean farmer had been working these food tunnels for a long time, making a decent living. But he was leasing the land they were positioned on, and he'd been notified that the price per month was going up. He'd concluded that the amount of increase would make the whole operation unprofitable for him, unless he could somehow scale up production by purchasing more tunnels. But he couldn't afford that kind of outlay, so he'd made the hard decision to sell off his overhead and look for another job.

Let me repeat, now, just for the record: *I am not a farmer.* Nothing about seeing these buckets of vegetables made me want to run put on a pair of coveralls and a Caterpillar hat. But the sheer magnitude of twenty thousand pounds of tomatoes hanging row by row in hundred-foot tunnels speaks to a certain volume of opportunity. And the entrepreneurial eyes in me saw the seed of a good idea.

I ended up spending two whole days following this farmer around, asking questions, taking notes, learning about crop rotations, gauging the price per kilo, tapping his brain for any information he might know about market timing and access, supply and demand.

By the time I got back to the States, I had brought home the makings of a comprehensive research project that was firing me up with excitement and potential. I dug up Internet data on wholesale prices and averages at Epping Market (which is a huge, HUGE, fresh-produce venue in Cape Town), as well as studying the websites of area grocery stores, getting a feel for their supply chains and corporate policies. After putting a pencil to how many cycles of vegetables we could realistically run through the tunnels, I came up with some conservative estimates, and calculated a detailed pro forma that showed a high likelihood for breaking even our first year out of the gate, laying the foundation for future expansion growth, and—most important—providing meaningful, life-skill employment to local workers.

Are missionaries allowed to have this much fun?

Should've thought of this years ago.

I went to Scott Harris at church and said, "For $15,000, Scott, we can buy two of these tunnels that are for sale, relocate them to the Living Hope campus, and earn enough money through the sale of cucumbers and tomatoes that the entire program could potentially wipe its face within a twelve-month period."

And guess what—we did! In fact, from this one-time capital investment, we actually turned a first-year *profit* of more than 20,000 rand (roughly $2,000 U.S. dollars) and were able to train three local people extensively through the platform, while employing a few more.

It worked!

Praise God.

And what amazed me—my part of it, at least—was that He had brought it about, not by turning me into a preacher, but by working through skills He'd already been cultivating in my life for years. Stuff I already enjoyed doing. How cool is that?

For example: John and I, through a member of his church who managed newspaper advertising for Food Lovers Market—a large grocery store chain, similar to our Whole Foods—got a chance to pitch our vegetables to their corporate buyer shortly after our permanent move to South Africa. Not many people get invited to that table, certainly not a little baling-wire outfit like ours.

We sat across from Valentino (yeah, are you intimidated yet?) at their main headquarters, while John began to tell them about the work of our ministry, how we operate as a nonprofit, serving the poor and yada yada. Good. Love the story. But this grocery guy, very politely and yet quite matter-of-factly, let us know he was really only interested in two things: the quality of our produce and the price. *If we could please hurry up and get to THAT* . . .

Man, I knew I was in my element then.

Reaching into my bag, I yanked out a wad of green beans that I'd grabbed, at John's request, on the way out the door, unwrapped them from the sleeve of newspaper I'd bundled them in, and laid it all out there in front of the food exec. He scooted forward in his chair, spread out the samples, examined their shape and color, rolled two or three of them around in his fingers, and said—just like that—"I'll take 100 percent of anything you grow that's this quality."

"It's *all* that quality."

"Sounds good, then."

"Perfect. Then how 'bout this . . ."

I was like a duck on a june bug now. I knew from my research that their company had implemented a five-year plan to reduce the carbon footprint of how they got their fruit and vegetable to market. So I surmised that being able to display our produce in their stores with a sticker or sign or something that said "Homegrown, Living Hope Tomatoes," could only help further their image as a socially conscious, earth-friendly business. Plus, people around here love what Living Hope does to alleviate poverty and social injustice, and they'd be drawn to that, even at a slightly higher price. Good for both of us. Good business.

"What I'd really like to do," I said, pressing the nego-tiations, "is to start with your two franchise locations that are closest to our tunnels. I understand they pay you five percent above market value to purchase from your own distribution center. I'd like to be able to go cut my own deal with their local management that would save *them* money, save us money, and provide you with the high-est quality goods you'll find anywhere, all while cutting down on the environmental costs of transportation and satisfying your green initiatives.

"But," I added, "I need you to bless it from the corpo-rate end, or they'll never return my phone calls."

Within a few months, we had a contract with their Tokai and Long Beach branches that saved each store 2.5 percent off what they paid their *own* headquarters for produce, and they had our guarantee that we would provide everyday delivery of tomatoes with crown and full-size cucumbers—all picked within twenty-four hours—and the option of expanding to sixteen other types of vegetables as our operation matures.

Now I could go get busy training and developing people.

We were off and running.

And see if you don't recognize God's fingerprints all over this deal—because as a result of this business transaction, white people in racially charged South Africa are now contributing to the economic uplift of black people, to the tune of more than fifty thousand cucumbers and forty thousand pounds of tomatoes so far. Christian, Muslim, pagan—makes no difference to me who's hungry and shopping. That's God's business. But money is flowing into the kingdom one healthy snack and salad ingredient at a time. And dozens of sharp individuals from the shacks of Masiphumelele (I'll help you pronounce it later) are being paid to work and learn at a profitable trade, all within a Christian discipleship environment that, I promise you, leaves us learning as much from them as they ever learn from us.

And some of them, as you'll see, are even going back to their homelands to start new businesses of their own. The journey out of tunnel vision continues.

Training Ground

The reality in South Africa—which I recognized early on—is that if a guy wants to improve himself educationally, if he truly wants to break the cords of abject poverty that keep his family tied down to subsistence living, one of the biggest problems is: *he can't afford to stop working to go do it.* A day spent in the classroom means a day he can't hire out his services, whatever little transient job he can find.

So we began to dream about a platform that could pay people while they learned viable job skills.

We are very serious at Living Hope and Living Way about not being just a handout-based charity. But we felt like, if people could meet certain qualifications, if we could run them through a selection process that indicated a baseline level of commitment and potential, we could make a significant, long-term impact on a healthy number of individuals. Could truly change the direction of their lives. For generations.

So by that summer—after sending out a letter to some friends—a number of generous donors supplied us with $20,000 for launching an agricultural and business academy, a multi-step program that takes qualified applicants through a full training curriculum in farming, business, community development, and base skills, completely infused with a Christian worldview. Richard Lundie, the general manager of Living Way, green-lighted the development of our coursework. And God, in His perfectly timed plans, sent us some business students from Samford

University in Birmingham, Alabama, to create the initial filtering sequence—a suite of fun, practical exercises designed to help us choose people who are most suited for growth and success. Those who are selected work half the week in the tunnels and spend the other half in the classroom. And throughout their tenure in the program, they earn a living wage for their efforts. That translates to food on the table for their families.

Basically, our academy is a three-tiered model, with the number of candidates being narrowed down as we go through the levels, but with achievement being awarded at the end of each phase, at each exit point. Those who complete the first phase, for example—the first three months—graduate with complete readiness for steady employment, having learned some common proficiencies that are taken for granted in some societies, but which are not often modeled in the cultures where many of these individuals come from. Things like computer skills, personal finance, timeliness, cleanliness, résumé development, productive study, and work habits.

You're probably thinking, "Hey, lots of people in America could use a refresher course in some of that stuff." (You're right! Might at least get 'em to pull their britches up, huh?) But armed with these basic elements of training, along with an introduction to various farming methodologies and business practices, every person in the program is celebrated at the end of the term for what they've accomplished.

Those who show greater competencies, however, and a desire for additional training proceed into Phase Two, which delves into more of the management side of things—the basics of building a business plan, how to delegate and supervise employees, how to gather and make decisions from useful information, how to analyze conditions in the community. Again, everyone who makes it through this part of the curriculum is graduated as a success, ready to go into contract farming, growing vegetables that can be sold into the market.

Then we reach the final phase—the entrepreneurial segment (my favorite!)—designed to extend for up to a full year, in which the students who show the most promise are given hands-on responsibility for running one of the tunnels as their own small business. They're faced with real-world challenges and are expected to respond in ways that keep their enterprise profitable. They manage risk, they diagnose problems, they tweak their processes, watch their costs, and plan their cash flow.

But more than just these essentials, they also learn to see themselves as contributors to the community at large, as a place of employment and opportunity for others, as a partner in raising the health and prosperity of their towns and villages and the families in these areas. Best of all, in addition to realizing the dream of owning their own business and farming operation, they're taught to see their company as *God's* business, with themselves as mere stewards of His gifts and resources. In this way, I'd say they're better prepared for success than millions of other entrepreneurs in the world (including the good ol' USA) who are just trying to score the big bucks.

When this third leg of the program is complete, there's one final condition: these entrepreneurial graduates cannot stay here at the ministry any longer. They must go back to their homes and begin implementing their business plans. They've brought to us their hearts and full lifetimes of knowledge; they've been taught skills and strategies that can foster a successful agricultural venture; and they've seen these techniques work in actual practice and economic conditions. Now it's their turn. And so they head out with our blessing and the loving support of our prayers and relationships—to honor God and extend the blessings of their Living Way training to their own families and neighborhoods.

All right, perhaps that's more than you wanted to know about our agricultural program. I understand that what I've described is very specific to our particular context. But it's just one very tangible example of the extraordinary things God can accomplish through surrendered, available hearts, even when we have no real idea what we're getting into at the beginning. What He started for me in a horse barn, giving me no other direction than just to follow Him, is now walking off the campus at Living Way as trained entrepreneurs. It's alive in the faces and embraces of new friends I am deeply privileged to know. Our lives are blended now. Forever. It blows my mind to think that something of me is being planted and cultivated right this minute in African soil somewhere, raised on African pastures, being prayed over in the field, and fed at family tables.

And sometimes I ask myself: That's what I was afraid to give up my "perfect" life for? That's the deep-down enjoyment I didn't think I could risk the security of my old job to experience? That's the feeling I was trading for a roomy office and a retirement package?

I watched our first three graduates, after the failure of a companion Living Way project raising chickens, come to me and say, "We know it failed, but we see the value of this program for the new group of students coming this summer." (Somebody had left the gate open, a dog got in, and killed all the livestock.) "So we want to give 300 rand apiece," they said, "from our own income to make sure they start out the new year with chickens."

They didn't have 300 rand ($30). *That's* not the way Africa operates. All that anybody expected them to say was, "If you ever try this again, be sure to double-check that the gate's closed at all times." Instead, their newly trained eye for service and opportunities that can benefit the community around them had driven them to proactive investment in others.

I looked at that and said, "Our work's done here. They get it. They're ready to go."

Life change.

You can't top it as a means for getting a cool rush of fulfillment.

I don't know if this agricultural training program is what I'll be doing for the rest of my life. It's certainly where God has put me for the time being. Three years from now, thirteen years from now, thirty years from now, I may still be doing this—or I may very well be doing something else. I may even be back in the States running a business again. Who knows? All I know is that I'm never going back to plotting my own flowchart of Joey Lankford's future. I'm never pinning myself down again to that kind of tunnel vision.

Whatever God chooses to do with me, I'm sure it'll be a whole lot better than anything I could've come up with. And as long as I know that, I'll just let Him be the one to decide where we go from here.

Afraid to Look

I'm convinced that one of the main reasons why people shy away from surrender—maybe you share this feeling—is the fear of not being able to see how things will come together on the back end. In just our one program alone, for example, there were so many details that went into it, so many people who were required, so many outside partnerships that were not originally in place, so many variables we couldn't possibly have foreseen or imagined before God put it all together.

But that's just the thing: *God puts it all together.* What makes us think that's so hard for Him to do? Why do we think He's all talk and no action?

Sure, you see what He's done with us, three or four years into our journey, and you think, "Well, yeah, I'd jump off if I knew I was landing someplace established like that, with all the kinks worked out." But don't kid yourself. We're not just winding it up and watching it go. Even though we did make a profit the first year, we're still growing and tweaking the platform every day. Like any business, we face new challenges all the time. We juggle the finances to keep it afloat. Nothing stays static and totally nailed down. Like I tell people all the time when I speak, we're still in the infancy stages of this process, still looking for new opportunities to grow and improve, to make it more effective and empowering. We still need people and skill sets that aren't here yet. Our plans and dreams still need money that hasn't been promised yet.

And my wife and children, outside of the whole Living Way thing entirely, still need His provision in areas we don't even *know* about yet! But like when our first rental house was sold out from under us—the story I told you about in an earlier chapter—I didn't even realize at the time how unsuitable for our family that first home was. I just thought I was dealing with life in Africa, forced to handle the same kind of allowances and make-dos that we'd need to accommodate no matter *where* we lived, anywhere else around here. But the place God found for us next, which took us from Kommetjie to Capri, is absolutely the perfect spot for us. And as if that's not enough blessing to handle, we're paying less in rent every month than we were before.

It's like this: with that kind of surrender comes that kind of freedom—the confidence of realizing that if you knew what God knew, if you could somehow possess His perfect vision of your situation, you would walk down this same exact path toward the unknown without a doubt that He will be there when you reach the next bend. If you knew what He knew, there's no way you'd settle for the simpler road, the more seemingly certain road.

The "devil" is not in the details. *God is!*

We keep walking through doors, and He keeps working out the process.

I hear from people just about every week who want to come over and volunteer with us—a horticulture major from Ole Miss, a nutrition student from the University of Tennessee, an engaged couple who want to come start working here together as soon as they're married in the spring. God has sent us one of the sharpest young CPAs I've ever met, a guy from Emory University in Atlanta, who spent a year getting his license with Deloitte and Touche. God has sent two young ladies who do curriculum development and lesson planning for the students— better candidates than I could have found if I'd gone out and handpicked them myself, women who love the Lord and want nothing else but to be of use to Him. God is putting our program together piece by piece, giving us exactly what we need.

And you know what's even more exciting? These people are discovering the same thing themselves, in their own lives. They heard all the conventional wisdom as they were growing up—how you go to school, get your degree, get the job, get the house. But they've watched their parents and the majority of other people they know—men and women who followed that advice and all the other standard expectations that go along with it—who are now shifting their money around in a desperate attempt to try holding on to what they've spent a lifetime working for. If that's what safety and security look like, then forget *THAT*—"Let's live life right now." And He is showing them (like He's showing me) what a sound investment His plan turns out to be.

They're stepping out on the possibilities, and filling up on His provision.

It's just how God responds to surrender.

Early on during some of our first days here, I climbed to the top of a mountain overlooking our house in Kommetjie, and felt like God gave me this prayer, which I set up on my computer so that it scrolls across the screen as an ongoing reminder, even to this day:

"Bless this endeavor beyond anything that could resemble human possibility."

Some stories, only God can write. Some plans, only God can create and staff and implement. If I could do it my way, I'd be the brains behind the outfit. I'd make it work and make it all about me. But you know what? You and I need to be in places where people look at what we're doing, and they say, *"You* could never have figured that out," because it's bigger than we are.

People with a hillbilly accent like mine shouldn't be walking into one of the largest fruit and vegetable retailers on the continent of Africa and getting clearance to do business with them. But God can. He's bigger than our worries, bigger than our flaws, bigger than our vision, and He knows how to show us where to take the next step so we remain in the flow of His blessing and fruitfulness. We don't need to know what that plan is or how He intends to pull it off. We only need to be here, trusting, following, expecting Him to turn our everyday efforts into something that's way more eternal.

Because He just wants us full and useful.

And so He needs us surrendered.

A True Tunnel Vision

As I said, not everything about our initial endeavor with the food tunnels was a whiz-bang success. In early March, the academy student whose innate farming brains and expertise had really laid the groundwork for the whole operation, a young man named Itai (pronounced it-TIE), returned to Zimbabwe temporarily—as an act of conscience and integrity—to settle some unresolved issues with his passport and identification papers. That left me taking his place for several weeks, just as the cucumber plants were beginning to bud.

I hadn't been in the tunnel more than twenty minutes, the Monday after his departure, than I noticed a bug infestation that needed some immediate attention. The next day, it was something else: our computerized irrigation system malfunctioned and lost all its settings. Took me forever to figure out how to reset it, meaning we had to resort to manually watering hundreds of plants while I brushed up on my problem-solving skills. At one point, to deal with some disease issues we'd encountered, we were forced to place some containers of disinfectant at the entrance to the greenhouses, where visitors were required to step on treated sponges before they entered the facility, hoping to stop the spread of contaminants.

Farming is tough.

Go ask a farmer.

But I'm telling you, God caused those little English cucumbers to really flourish. At times, if I could've spared an hour just to sit on a five-gallon bucket and watch them, I swear I would've have been able to both see and hear them grow. The lushness of the plants, the quality of the product, the rapid rate of growth toward harvest . . . incredible.

Everybody was amazed. Like me.

A short while later, as the time came for our tomatoes to ripen, we started to get set up on a Tuesday morning to pick the ones that were ready for selling. But I noticed, walking in and out of the greenhouses and taking care of other business, that nobody was picking anything. "What's the matter?"

Itai walked over to me and said, "The men refuse to pick any tomatoes until you walk through the tunnel and pray over it."

Well, I appreciated that. I really did. Sure, we should pray. But sometimes, you know, in the heat of the day's action, you can look at situations that, yes, technically call for the same spiritual consistency you've been practicing and preaching about, like the way we'd prayed over the planting of initial seeds in each of the bags, and yet . . . come on, y'all, can't we just get busy here? We're burning daylight.

I was frankly a bit surprised at how seriously they were taking this matter. They obviously weren't kidding. They weren't willing to pick the first tomato until I'd walked the perimeter with them, up and down the rows, asking God's blessing on these fruits of their (and His) labor—as if, you know, prayer wasn't just a Christian formality, as if prayer really made a difference.

Weird, huh? I know.

Itai said, "We watched you walk through the cucumber tunnel and pray over it before we picked, and we've witnessed God's blessing on it. We will wait until you do the same thing for the tomato tunnel."

Gosh. And here I was, thinking (on some days, when I *wasn't* thinking) that the success of our little enterprise was measured in factors of harvest quantities, in the number of impoverished individuals we were putting to work, who were helping us turn this idea of ours into a viable business model. And dog-gone if these African laborers weren't shaking me out of my bean-counting mentality to remind me that I was actually here on *other* business.

God's business.

I believe I can honestly say, I never prayed so fervently, passionately, and downright believingly over any morsel of food as I prayed that morning over those come-to-Jesus tomatoes. I don't know if my prayers put any kind of extra blush on their plump, red faces, but the Lord sure did some reviving in my own heart as I asked Him to pour down His favor on their taste and freshness and their upcoming travels to market.

Truly, there is so much more to life than what we try to make of it by putting our heads down and plowing ahead with the best energy we can muster.

A shop owner across the street saw that in a cucumber.

My guys and I saw it that morning in our tomatoes.

I hope I never lose sight of it myself, ever again.

Chapter 7

A World Connected

never wanted to be a missionary.

I don't even like the word.

Missionary.

Makes me think of the people who'd come through church every so often when I was younger, dressed kind of funny, showing their slides, standing around with their goofy kids in the vestibule trying to make us taste seaweed or something. *No thanks, we already ate.*

Pssh.

Never crossed my mind that I'd ever end up trending that way myself. "Joey the missionary." In fact, there was a time not too long ago, I'm ashamed to say, when I would've been embarrassed to tell people this is what I did for a living. (Of course, if I'd have known missionaries could wear T-shirts, camo pants, and a Big Orange ball cap to work, I might have heard the call a lot sooner!)

But I think people have gotten the message these days that missions is a lot more than preaching on a street corner or sitting around studying the Bible all day in grass huts. Nothing wrong with any of that, naturally, and I'm thankful to God for the people whose main job is to go house to house, anywhere in the world, just talking about Jesus. But from what I've seen and experienced of missions, it doesn't usually take you a million miles away from whatever you're already good at, or from whatever job you could imagine yourself doing if you could do anything you wanted. It's not like the difference between being who you are today and being an astronaut. Missions work doesn't live on a whole other planet from the vocational or interest areas that are already inside you. (I'll talk a little more specifically about that in an upcoming chapter.)

And yet, like I said, while I believe people are starting to get this message—which was news to me when I first heard it—I think what's been the most surprising thing to me about missions is that it's not so tightly confined to the official task a person is here to do. Whatever that particular job is—in my case, fostering entrepreneurism among the impoverished in South Africa—the assignment very soon takes a back seat to the part that does most of the life-changing work.

And this is the part that moves the "missionary" target outside of just the African bush and perhaps draws it within range of the bushes outside your own house or apartment complex. When you think about what it means to be a missionary, the key ingredient is not "location, location, location"—it's "surrender, surrender, surrender." Every believer who truly grasps what the gospel means, both for themselves and others, and who yields their plans and desires to the Lord, refusing to captain the ship of their lives any longer, that person becomes a missionary wherever they are. Being a missionary is simply what happens when a living relationship with the living God leads you into living relationships with others.

Missions is all about relationships.

It's about living with people. Sharing with people. Listening to people. Learning from people. Interacting with people. Eating with people. Serving people. Encouraging people.

I've often thought, even when doing something as ordinary as digging a garden plot next to a young African villager, how the simple act of working alongside another person is enough all by itself to develop a relationship. You'll talk. Things will come up. You'll solve problems together. Your histories and memories will cross. Life will pass between you, and God will do what only God can do—bless that personal connection with gospel significance.

Same goes for you, wherever you live, whatever you do. It's what Paul was getting at, I think, when he said to a group of people in one of the churches he started, "We cared so much for you that we were pleased to share with you not only the gospel of God but also our own lives" (1 Thess. 2:8). The gospel is so much more than a sermon outline or a bunch of biblical bullet points. It's as real as human need and as hopeful as a genuine smile and a belly laugh. It's as intimate as a back porch conversation and as everyday as a coffee break. The opportunities for doing missions work are all around you, all the time . . . because *people* are around you all the time.

And again, I don't mean thinking of people as if they were gospel marks, using your relationship with them as a tactical maneuver to lower their resistance to the Christian message so you can hopefully reel them in when you spot them ready to bite. No, I'm just talking about loving people and getting to know them, moving toward them, looking for them, listening for where they hurt, being a friend, becoming involved enough in others' lives until you truly understand who they really are, letting them see you up close as a broken person yourself, rescued by the grace and mercy of God.

So while the pragmatic Western capitalist in me wants to define my life in terms that can fill out an impressive PowerPoint presentation—and while even the missionary mind in me says that I should be measuring trends and percentages and counting the noses of how many folks we're helping on an average day—God just continues drawing me back into real-life orbit with the people and relationships right around me. And as a result, merely by the way His kingdom works, He keeps showing up with the most awesome, honest experiences of abundant life I've ever known.

He's changing lives, right here in front of me, right where I can see them.

And the life He's changing the most is mine.

Crossing the Divide

Being introduced to those tunnels that day—my first day in South Africa—was the beginning of a new business proposition for Living Way. Little did I realize it was also the beginning of new friendships that would enrich my life and my family's lives with all the colors of another culture, while also positioning me for a level of one-on-one ministry I honestly didn't know I was capable of doing.

Itai (I spoke about him at the end of the last chapter) lost his job the day we bought the greenhouses. He had been working with the farmer who ran them—Sarel Vermaak—until our purchase officially put that operation out of business. And as we began the process of dismantling those structures for relocation to our property, we brought in some of the people who'd already been employed through our ministry to help us do it. But one of the guys didn't show up one day. And Sarel pointed to a slight, slender Zimbabwean man standing under a nearby shade tree, and said, "You can have *him*, if you want him."

Never in a million years would I have thought someone who looked so unwanted could become so indispensable to our work in the food tunnels. His instinctive knack for crop production, his tireless work ethic, and his eagerness to learn and grow through the various challenges we faced would prove instrumental to all the success we enjoyed in our initial rounds and rotations of vegetable farming. What an amazing guy!

But more than anything, Itai and I became best buds. He's back in his home country now, working out his business plan, trying to start a productive chicken farm and supporting his wife and two kids as one of our first three graduates from the academy. And this is no lie when I say it: wherever I happen to be on planet earth, at any point in my lifetime, if Itai called to say he needed my help, I would drop whatever I was doing and go there. Right then. He'd do the same thing for me, if he could. I know it. How many friends do any of us have who really mean that?

But our relationship didn't grow this tight without incident. In fact, had it not been for a couple of very tense relational sequences between us, I don't know that we'd be the brothers we've become. God has a way of using the messy moments we share with others to become the mortar that rubs against our sharp edges and differences until we're ultimately glued together, inseparable.

Pammzy, a Malawian who worked with us, was just beginning to drive away from the tunnels one afternoon with Itai, heading out on a tomato delivery, when I—snap decision, very last second—decided my tired old bones could use the quarter-mile lift to the main building where they (and I) were headed. So without even hollering to tell them I was hopping on, I just plunked my rear end on the back of the truck bed, letting my legs and feet dangle from the lowered gate.

All of a sudden, we lurched to a stop, and Itai came tumbling out of the passenger door, "Joey, you need to get up front."

"Huh? No, I was just catching a ride up the hill. I'm getting off here in just a second. Don't worry about it."

"No, I—I can't ride up there."

"What do you mean? Why *can't* you?"

"I, uh . . . uh . . ."

Ohhh. I get it.

"It's because I'm white and you're black. Is that it?"

He wouldn't even raise his eyes to meet mine, or even to try voicing an answer. Just stood there. Head down. Paralyzed, like, *please*, I wasn't possibly going to make this any more uncomfortable for him than it already was, *am I?*

And I mean, the Holy Spirit in that moment just blew back any confusion I'd registered at first and showed me exactly what was happening here. And then, as if I'd been given a script to read, shoved into my hands from stage left, I launched right into a real-life parable of sorts to get my point across.

Yes, I knew Itai and Pammzy were in a hurry, but I was calling time-out. We were stopping to deal with this. Right here.

"Let me tell you something, Itai. Up at our home in Kommetjie, we don't have any heat. It gets pretty cold at night. So we let Bristol—you know Bristol—we let her sleep in the room at the top of the stairs where most of the heat from the fireplace goes. She's the smallest, and that's where she can stay the warmest. You got me?

"Now if I understand what you're asking, if I was to apply this same logic of yours at home, I'd need to go wake up Bristol tonight, get her out of bed, and tell her—*because she's black*—she can't sleep in that warm room anymore, that I'm putting one of my other kids there, just because they're white. Is that what you're saying?"

Still no visible response.

Well, I wasn't standing around there all day till he got the message. "Itai, *get* back in the truck! *I'm* riding back here!" I turned away from him, slid myself back onto the drop-down gate again, and sat there like a statue, facing the other way.

White guys may not jump, but I'd jumped him pretty good.

I heard him slowly get in. Shut the door.

Very reluctantly.

But it crawled all over him. That's just not the way it's done in South Africa. You don't see white men ever looking subservient to a black man in any way. You don't see white men working manual labor, not when black Africans are all over the place who'll do anything at all for a few rand—cart your groceries across the parking lot, watch your car while you're inside, come up to your house, trim your bushes, water your flowers.

And I can tell you for sure, you *never* see a white man on the back of a truck that a black man is driving.

Our little hop and a skip down the road took no more than thirty seconds, tops. But the impact of what it meant and how it felt to Itai stuck with him for weeks on end. Several months later, in fact, after our family had already been home to America for a long summer furlough and were back in Africa again—after all that time—he was assigned one morning to lead our team devotional. Every one of the Living Way staff was there. And the theme he chose to address was his take on the slave and master teaching of the Bible, which he summarized by looking at me—with big, heavy tears in his eyes, his face all gritted up—saying, "I can't be your worker and also be your friend." To read his body language, it was as if he was saying, "I feel like I want to, but I can't." His culture, his history, it all said no.

I wanted to just sit there and hurt for him. I really did. Feel sorry for him. Who wouldn't? But what came out instead was, I guess, the one challenge that God must have known he needed to hear from me, because I sensed deep in my spirit it was what I needed to say. And as harsh as it may have sounded, I hoped he would understand it came from love.

"You can't be my friend?" I said. "Then you need to get up and leave."

Total quiet. The only sound was the battle of dueling worlds, club-fighting inside his own head.

"I'm not here to be your master, Itai, I'm here to love you. You can't work for me anymore if you can't be my friend."

Everybody was crying by then.

But I learned something extremely valuable through this interaction. I discovered that my main job here is not to raise cucumbers, or even to raise the economic hopes of the poor and disadvantaged in Africa. My main missionary task is to be in personal relationship with men like Itai—iron sharpening iron—people who teach me while I'm teaching them, and who in the process become my friends and fellow laborers in Christ.

Itai may have needed me to oversee his work for a brief season of his life. He may have needed me to show him how to provide a viable, sustainable, marketable outlet for his farming efforts. But what he really needed to see, more than anything, was somebody who loved him, who lived the gospel with him, and who would be there for him—like when I was kicking open the door in the hospital while his son was in the emergency room having a seizure, with me telling the medical staff in no uncertain terms *this kid is dying out here!*

"Just have a seat, sir."

"Have a seat? Have you seen this kid?"

"We're busy with other patients right now, sir. You'll just need to—"

Yeah. With patients from around here. Not a little foreign, Zimbabwean boy like this one, huh? He'll just have to wait, right? "No, I'm not going anywhere. Look! At him!"

And when she finally did, she could see. We were losing him. They took him back, treated him, he's fine now.

But that's the reality of life for Itai, and for millions more like him. Do they need financial help, business help, marketing help, planning help? Of course they do. And we give it every day. But what that black man living in South Africa needed most from me was a friend—a friend he didn't think he could have, a friend who wasn't supposed to look and talk like I do, a friend who should have just known without being told that he belonged up in the truck cab, not riding around like loose dirt in the back of a pickup.

That's what being a missionary is. Living shoulder to shoulder. Standing up for people who need the added weight of our defense and protection. Walking out the journey as friends, even with all of our personal wounds and blemishes exposed, our imperfections, right out where people can see them.

It changes lives.

It'll change *you*.

Can I Help You?

I was out in the drizzling cold of an ugly day, digging a drainage ditch with one of our employees, Godfrey, who'd been working with me for several months. I was taking a quick breather beside a fence post while he kept shoveling nonstop. What a worker! Finally I said, just because I'd never asked, "Godfrey, you've never really told me a lot about your family. You married?"

"Yes, yes, I am. And we have a baby girl. She's two and a half."

"Oh, yeah? Really?"

"But I haven't been able to go back to them since I came down here to find work three years ago. The first two years, I was working day labor—just enough to get by and keep sending them money, but not enough for travel. And even still, even now, I can't—"

"Wait," I said, doing a little Tennessee math in my head. "You've been here three years? And your daughter's two and a half?"

"Yes."

"You mean, you've never . . . seen her?"

He went back to digging. "No." Trying not to think about it. "No, I haven't."

Give that answer of his a second to land on you—a father who adored his little daughter, but had never laid eyes on her.

Sarel was working with us that day. For the first six months after we'd bought his tunnels from him, he had gone to work with a startup business. But once that job had played out, he came over to Living Way to help with our agricultural program. I'm so glad he did. Sarel has taught me so much, not only about farming but also about life and contentment and serving others. But like nearly everybody else who's been born and raised in this culture, his life as a white man has been unavoidably influenced by the racial feelings and fabric here. That's what made it even more encouraging when I heard him reach out to Godfrey with a generous question: "How much would it cost you to get home and back, to get your family here?"

"2,100 rand." (About $250.)

"Tell you what," Sarel said, "if you can save up 700 rand yourself, I'll give you another 700."

"And I'll match it," I jumped in. "That'd give you the 2,100 you need."

And Godfrey did it—as hard as I've ever seen anyone work. "I've got my 700 rand, Mr. Joey," he told me one day. *Perfect, here's mine.* And not too long after that, I was sitting in my office one morning when he showed up in the doorway, beaming like he'd just won the lottery. His wife and daughter had arrived by bus the night before, and here they were, all together as a family. For the *first . . . time . . . ever.*

"Joey, meet Brenda," he said.

I knelt down to her three-year-old level to say hello—looking into a pair of beautiful, chocolate eyes that her own father had not even seen until about eight hours before—and thought, *What else could I buy for $80 that would do this for me?*

Wouldn't you think a feeling like that should at least cost as much as a big-screen television? Maybe even an in-ground swimming pool, a kitchen remodel, a new Toyota? But instead, God had walked an abundant life experience right through my door, and it hadn't cost me as much as a week's groceries.

Think of that.

Five loaves, two fish. Why should we be so shocked to know that God can take a small investment in one relationship, and watch Him work multiplication miracles through it? Besides, I'd just seen him do it in another friend's life, not a few months before.

Clifford and I had met during my very first solo week in South Africa at the church where John Thomas preaches. Impressive guy. Didn't know anything about him, of course, but when we set up our academy the following season, he applied and was accepted.

He, too—like Itai—was originally from Zimbabwe, but had fled to South Africa for work opportunities under the threat of political persecution that was brewing against his parents and clan. He'd actually earned a diploma in tourism and leisure management, but the conditions in his homeland had deteriorated to the point that his only prospects for employment lay elsewhere. Through his hard labor in and around Cape Town, eventually with Living Way and our job-creation initiative, he was able to support his wife and children back home.

Clifford was a natural for our entrepreneurial program. He rose through the levels into our final mentoring phase, framing up his business plan for the pig farm he's now gone back to start. But even though our ministry became like a family to him, nothing could completely alleviate his loneliness for home—especially when he received word that his wife had been diagnosed with an advanced stage of breast cancer. Very deadly. Very serious.

What I want you to see in Clifford's story is not Joey. I was just a bit player. What I want you to see are missionary hearts, reaching out for relationships—some over here in South Africa, some back in America—some working in full-time ministry capacities like me, some working their same old jobs or raising kids at home—but everybody tuned in to needs and people and possibilities and the kingdom.

Missionaries.

Active missionaries.

Clifford told me about his wife and her sickness. It was hard to hear. Hard to imagine. What would I do if that was Courtney? Fifteen hundred miles away? Sick and dying with no money for surgery and treatment and no husband at home to lean on, to cry with, to care for her?

I didn't tell him, but I mentioned Clifford and his wife's problems to a buddy of mine, Allen West, who's a member of our Sunday school class back home. Just asked them to be praying. Thanked them for caring for us so well and being such a huge part of what we're trying to do over here. Allen shared with everybody what I'd told him, how a precious family in Zimbabwe was suffering this level of heartache and hopelessness and desperation, a family who in God's bloodline was connected to our church and class through Courtney and I, half a world away . . . *What would the Lord want us to do?* he asked.

Tate and Brooke Elder also became involved, once they heard it. (You remember their story I told you in chapter 5.) They were still back home at the time, dealing with their own call to missions, and they began e-mailing notes of encouragement and prayer to Clifford, while keeping everybody else in the class updated on what was going on.

About a month later, I met Allen at the Cape Town airport. We drove out together from our house the next day to the tunnels. I introduced him to Clifford—just telling him this guy was a pal of mine who'd come over from America to see us. And, oh yeah, he's brought a little something for you as well—a check for $2,500, pooled together very sacrificially by the forty couples in our class who wanted to be sure Clifford's wife had her surgery and her chemo treatments and her husband by her side . . . whatever she needed so she could live.

Clifford's such a bright guy. Sharp. Articulate. Funny. A strong presence. Always something to say. But this was too much. There wasn't really any compartment in his brain and in his background where he could file away an amount of generosity this large, where he could grasp what God had given him through a surprise relationship with brothers and sisters from a land he'd never set foot on. And except for the tears leaking from the corners of his eyes, he couldn't get much else out of his system except a whisper . . . a thank you.

Overwhelmed. Wow.

Talk about a moment.

Actually, let me make a correction. That part about the "land he'd never set foot on" isn't true anymore, because the following year, God opened the logistical door for Clifford to obtain an unlimited travel visa (a quite miraculous story all by itself), and to book a flight to America during the part of the summer when my family and I were already over there. This meant that on one incredible Sunday in Brentwood, Tennessee, he was able to join us during our class period at church to express his and his wife's gratitude to all of us in person for the money they'd been given, and to celebrate her recovery from cancer because of what my friends had done in response to God's leading.

Now—what do you think our class time was like that day? Think we just sat around reading out of our Sunday school books? Think we were fidgeting our feet, crossing our legs, covering our yawns, wondering how much longer it was going to be till the closing prayer? Do you think anybody in attendance that morning was disappointed in the return on their $50 investment?

No, we all just sat there in amazement of how good it feels to be full. Not wanting to leave. And when we did, what do you think we each carried out the door with us but another stack of stones to remind us what God can do with surrendered hearts.

This is what He wants for us, people. For *all* of us. He wants us full. Fulfilled. Rolling around in abundant life until we don't know if we can take it anymore. Experiencing the blessing of interacting with others in ways only He could orchestrate. Meeting needs, learning to love, developing lifelong friendships and unforgettable memories of His goodness.

That's missions.

Around the world, and right here at home.

People loving people in Jesus' name—and being filled up to the brim by what God does in the process.

Life Together

I don't know where I'm catching you today. I don't know what you're feeling or thinking as you hear about our story and the stories of other people we've gotten to know. All I can tell you is that if life is feeling sort of empty and dry these days, one of the best moves you'll ever make is to open yourself up to a new level of surrender toward God, and start intentionally connecting your life with other people on this new journey you're taking with Him.

If you're not sure where to begin, just start with the people right around you. Like your neighbors. You don't need to rehearse some kind of gospel spiel to give them. Could you just go over and say hello? Introduce yourself? Would that be so scary? Would it hurt you to push through this one wall of resistance you feel, if you do, and just see what God might make of it?

Honestly, I didn't do so well with this simple courtesy when I was back in the States. I was busy as all get-out and too wrapped up in my own little world to even go across the street and see who lived there. I wonder, though, how seriously God ever took some of my big promises about being sold-out to Him and all interested in serving Him when He'd already plopped me right in the middle of a neighborhood full of people that I obviously couldn't care less about.

The first neighbor I really got to know well in my whole life is the one who lives three doors down from us now, right here in South Africa. Isn't that crazy? And the first time I saw him, he was beating the tar out of two young guys who were fishing through our trash—looking for American treasure, I guess.

Everybody, meet Mike.

"They were wanting in your house," he yelled, as he marched up our front walk. "I hid in the bushes and listened to them talking. They were casing your place. Thought I'd better take care of them for you."

"Well, thanks, man," I said, sounding very green, feeling way out of my element. "I see we've got a lot to learn about living here."

And we've sure learned a ton from Mike. Or as my kids have come to call him, *Uncle* Mike.

Mike's a commercial fisherman. If that doesn't conjure up an image for you, think truck driver. The gnarliest kind you can imagine. Rougher than a goat's knees. All sweat and hair and smell and beer. As my little boy Barron says, he "has fish on him." Or at least that's what he told me the Sunday morning when he said he didn't want to go to church, that he wanted to stay home with Uncle Mike. "Why do you think Mike doesn't go to church?" I asked him.

"Because he has fish on him."

There's a lot of theology in that simple statement, I think, for a little fellow. And a lot of dressed-up church-goers trying to cover the smell of fish on themselves with all that detergent and cologne. Note to self: It's not working.

So, yeah, I don't think it would surprise you to know that Mike doesn't put a lot of stock in our religious beliefs. But we've welcomed him into our home and into our lives all the same. And though he doesn't let a lot of people get too close to him, he's welcomed us into his life as well.

We're buddies, Mike and me. I'm just real with him. And as a result, he's real with me. Loves my kids. And loves that my kids love him.

One day, in fact, I was out fishing with Mike on his boat—out in the Atlantic—when another boat pulled up alongside us. It was Gray.

Gray is, uh . . . honestly, without seeing him yourself, there's no way I can adequately describe to you the sheer horror and evil that comes out of every pore of that man's body. I swear I'm not overdramatizing for effect. He's a Rasta-kind of guy, a colored man, white dreads. He is one of *THE* official drug lords of Ocean View, a hotbed for crime, gang activity, and tik addiction—the South African name for crystal meth. Not the kind of person you mess with. We'll often see him just sitting in his white truck, stoned out of his mind, maybe at a red light or something, and I'll tell the kids, "Just look forward. Don't look over there, whatever you do." Demons snarling all over him. You can see it in his eyes.

Midnight-movie scary.

You've probably never seen anything like it. *I* sure hadn't.

We were hauling in crayfish nets when Gray rocked by and started jawing with Mike in Afrikaans. I had no idea what either one of them were saying. But then I saw Mike reach down and toss him a mess of fish heads. I figured Gray and his ghastly crew must've just been looking for bait.

But then he looked straight at me, and said in his heavily accented English, "What are you doing with that black kid in your car?"

My brain said, *You touch her, man, and I'll*—mmmh!—but my mouth gave a much smarter, much more concise answer: "I adopted her."

"She not from here?"

"No. She's from Ethiopia."

At that, he went to speaking Afrikaans again, back and forth with Mike for a second, then turning around to holler something to the other men in his boat, pointing back at me, gesturing, slithering through his words. *What's going on here?* I was thinking. This was creeping me out. Finally, his boat fired up, they started to pull away, but not before he sneaked one more evil-eye glance in my direction. "See you, bro," he said.

Oh, Lord, "Mike, man, what was that?"

"You don't know what he said, do you?"

"No. What?"

"He said, 'I've seen him in his green car with that black baby. Is he a good guy?' I said, 'Yeah, he's my neighbor. 12 Main Road.' 'Good dude?' he asked. 'Yeah,' I said, 'good dude.' That's when he looked around at everybody else in his boat, and said, 'Make sure word gets out in Ocean View—nobody messes with 12 Main Road. You hear me? Nobody.'"

Dang, man.

My spirit did a little flutter. I couldn't believe what I'd just heard. Couldn't wait to get home and tell Courtney how the Lord had signed us up that afternoon for a whole-house protection plan, using the most wicked of all to bless the righteous.

I pass Gray now sometimes, and he'll say to me something like, "Need some lobster for your family tonight?" then he'll fling me a sackful of fresh catch. You kidding me? Is this really happening? Having Gray looking out for my wife and kids? But it's all because of a relationship built with Mike, just being together, loving him for who he is, being there for him when he needs me.

Like the Sunday night he called me up, asked if I could come over. *Sure.* I get over there, and he's been in the sauce a little bit. Kind of mellowed out. Oddly emotional.

"Dude," he said, right off the bat, "you know the way you guys live? Religion and all that? I don't have time for that [bleep]." He trailed down that road for a little bit, while I sat there listening, figuring he must be going somewhere with it, or else he could've just had this little conversation by himself. "You know my dad?" he said. "Across the road?"

"Wait, no, Mike. Your dad? Lives here on this street? No, I didn't know that."

"Yeah," he said, a lost, lonely look starting to float across his eyes. Then he proceeded to tell me a story about how, when he was twelve years old, he saved up enough money selling crayfish, pennies at a time, until he was finally able to buy something he'd always wanted: his own surfboard. The first day he bought it, he took it out into the ocean and stayed way up into the afternoon. Young kid, new toy.

Mike's father had one rule, he said: "Be home before the sun goes down." And on that one particular, first full day with his brand-new surfboard, Mike was just a few minutes past dark getting home. Not an hour late, just barely late, the way Mike remembers it. But his dad snatched that surfboard from under his arm, took it out in the backyard, and hacked it into sharp, jagged pieces with a chain saw, then lit fire to it and burned it into ash. I have no reason to think he's making that up.

"And I hate that [blankety-blank] today more than anybody else on the planet," he said.

By this time, I'm just sitting there, not knowing what to do. *Why is he telling me this? What does he want me to say?* And yet I just waited. Quiet. Looking down at first, then looking up again, staring him in the eye. The mood was heavy. Too heavy to speak into it.

FULFILLED

"Then this morning," he broke back in, "there was a preacher from your country on the radio as I was getting out of the shower. And he was talking about forgiveness. *Forgiveness!*" He chuckled a little, then got deathly serious again. "He said the feeling I have inside of me, by not forgiving my dad for what he did and for what he's done, is hurting me more than it hurts him.

"Is that true, Joey? Is that true?"

If you were waiting for a sinner's prayer report at the end of this story, I'm sorry, I don't have one. Don't have what you're looking for. What I said to him was just one friend talking truth to another friend at a pivotal moment in his life. But Courtney and I know—without a doubt!—God is reeling this man in for His kingdom. Slowly but surely. He's set the hook and is just waiting for my buddy to wear himself out before He pulls him on in. I'm convinced we'll see Mike Smith in heaven, saved and repentant and blessed and forgiven. But in the meantime, I just keep sharing life with him. The good days, the bad days. The rotten Joey days and the fully surrendered days.

That's what missionaries do.

They build relationships. Real ones.

And then God does the rest.

I do it here in South Africa.

Where do *you* do it?

Chapter 8

Keep It Simple

About two years into our missionary adventure, Courtney and I packed up the kids for a ten-day getaway into the African bush.

Think safari terrain. Lots of tall, thick grass. Wide-open spaces and *Lion King* sunsets. A place where you can hear the hoots and howls of exotic wildlife ricocheting from one end of the night sky to the other.

Sounded like a pretty cool vacation spot to me.

And we did have big fun. We relaxed. We chilled. Did whatever we wanted. While I'm sure the fanny-packed tourists back home were snaking through hour-long lines to sit for two or three minutes on the Jungle Cruise—shoot, we were making our bed right out there in the middle of it, all day every day, for a full week and a half. And we weren't paying no fifteen dollars a pop for a theme-park pretzel and a watered-down Coke either.

I'd say it was a good deal all around.

But on Day Six of our little summer sabbatical, I decided I was going even deeper into the native habitat. I drove out by myself in our old rattletrap Land Rover, going about as far into the middle of nowhere as I think I'd ever been, just to do some praying and listening and thinking out loud. After finally pulling to a stop at the edge of a remote, shady patch of road—nobody anywhere around—I settled in for what I hoped to be a long, undisturbed stretch of devotional time.

My Bible and journal were out and open in front of me. My mind was working to stay quiet and focused. And even though a stiff, dry African breeze was cross-ventilating through the car windows, even though the sights and smells all around me left no doubt which part of the world I was in, I could almost imagine for a moment—if I closed my eyes real tight and took a deep breath—that I was back in a certain horse barn in the dead of a Tennessee winter. Fire crackling in the stove. Musty sweetness of cut hay in the air.

Because the longer I sat, the more clearly I could sense God's presence—much like the way I'd sensed it on that one-and-only Saturday night, the night that had kick-started what ultimately led me to this place, to this moment, to a new home on a new continent.

I think He wanted to make sure I was keeping the two together.

After twenty-four months of a new normal—even *this* kind of normal, one that at first had been totally foreign to us, way outside of our typical box—life had done what life does: consistently complicate things, continually do battle against a man's contentment. I had thought maybe that by moving away with God to South Africa, I'd fix the part of myself that resisted being satisfied, that I'd be done with some of those same struggles and tendencies I'd battled for so long. But, no, they were still here, even this far away from home, even this long into our missionary experience. All they'd done was find a different backdrop, a new set of circumstances to work with. And on some days, they were doing a really good job of gunking up my entire system.

For example, I'd been trained by my American roots to thrive on movement, progression, and incremental growth, always juggling a dozen things at once, afraid to ever sit still, for fear I might miss an opportunity. So I had brought over with me to Africa not only my excitement and energy for missions and business thinking, but also a results-oriented paradigm that basically just came with the package. It's how we operate, right? *Get 'er done.*

And while there's certainly plenty to be gained from this kind of drive and ambition, there's also the possibility that a lot of it is just a cover for insecurity, not to mention a lack of trust in God and in His timing. What's more, it can affect the way we relate to others, especially at work, keeping our heads so full of business details and production deadlines, we lose sight of the people we're doing it all with. We forget they're not just puzzle pieces for us to plug into our developmental goals.

That was *part* of what God was showing me.

But there was more. Even though He had definitely given me much more freedom to follow Him without needing to ask so many questions, to recognize His voice and to move accordingly, I was still a long way from being completely certain He wasn't going to let a ball drop somewhere and leave us up a creek. I mean, sure, I had learned from many new and recent experiences that His provision somehow had always come together in our lives. The stones had kept stacking. He'd made sure of that. But I still couldn't seem to completely let go of my obsession for making plans, for wanting to figure out my future, needing to draw it up with spreadsheets and decimal points and directional arrows.

I know it's natural of us—and it's wise, up to a point—to think ahead, to crunch the numbers, to eliminate as many uncertainties and contingencies from our lives as possible. But how often do we go into planning mode simply because we're freaking out at what might happen—and at what's *not* happening? We want to know what's going on. We want to know as much as *God* knows. And we want to see it on paper.

So as I thought back that afternoon on the past two years, I could feel some pushback in my spirit from these two old, familiar holdouts: a restlessness for going faster, higher, stronger—maybe *too* fast, *too* high, *too* strong—as well as my habitual stress about our family and personal matters, from the petty and everyday to the much more major and long-range.

But even *that* wasn't all—because whenever I wasn't feeling the tug of these distractions, there were always those moments when things were going *great* . . . which are sometimes every inch the monster that our worries and impatience can be.

In the past year, for instance, I'd started blocking out two full mornings a week, 9:30–12:30, to conduct tours of our campus for church groups and other nonprofits, folks who'd heard about some of the things that were going on at Living Way and wanted to come see our work for themselves. In addition, a film production crew had been over here from the States a few months back to create a full-length documentary highlighting our ministry and its impact on the poor and needy. People were buzzing me every day on social media, asking for just five or ten minutes of Skype time, wanting to know any way they could be involved with us, what they could send to us, who they could connect with us, how they could sponsor us.

And that's good. That's *great*!

Hope I'll be hearing from *you* soon, in fact.

But I'm sure you know what I'm talking about—the change that can subtly begin to happen when your in-box is filling up, when your ego is being stroked, when people are coming around you all the time to tell you how great you are, how impressed they are, how they want to take you to meet this person and that person, how bright the future looks for somebody with your kind of potential and skill set.

Hear enough of that, and you can start to think they're right.

Must be pretty good being me, huh? Look what Joey's done. Couldn't have done it without Joey. Y'all know about Joey? "Of course we know Joey. He's that guy who went to Africa and everything."

Yeah . . .

Joey: The World Tour.

I'm sure God was really impressed.

And so those are just a few of the reasons why sitting there in the front seat of my dusty, old Defender on that December summer day, I could sense Him sort of firing up the rooter machine again, needing to clean out my clogged pipes. As the hours passed, and as the stillness began settling even more perceptibly around me, all that stuff I've been telling you about began to glug up out of my heart—two years' worth of buildup from various pressures and doubts, along with whatever amount of buildup I'd been wanting to believe about myself, about my own personal brand. It all started coming dislodged from where it had been latched on and hiding, down where it had been clogging my arteries, doing its damage.

And in that deep-cleansing moment, a very clear, refreshing thought rushed into those newly scrubbed, empty spaces, as though God was quietly trying to say to me, "Come on, son, let's get back to the barn."

Back to those feelings.

Back to believing in Me.

Back to being in love with Me.

Back to everything being *about* Me.

Back to not needing to know it all, and yet knowing all you need to know. Back to not having anything more important to do today than just being ruggedly obedient to whatever I show you. Back to living in total faith and trust and availability. Back—all the way back . . .

To surrender.

Now you'd think a missionary would already know this, wouldn't need to be told again and reminded of it. But let's just pull back the blinds for a second, the ones that we artificially place between us and people who do certain kinds of Christian work for a living, and hear me say, loud and clear: *my faith is every bit as likely to be forgetful as yours is.* Nothing about changing my mailing address changed the fact that I'm still quite capable of carrying around a lot of old perspectives on life, on God, and on myself that are broken and out of whack. The things I consider to be my basic needs, my normal expectations for how life is supposed to go, how people are supposed to treat me, stuff like that—I'm always subject to reverting back to the way I used to perceive it all, to the lies I apparently still want to believe sometimes.

We're pretty much the same, you and me.

Missionary or not.

But every time we do it, every time we force ourselves to learn the same stupid lessons over and over again—just because of how dense and fearful and fickle we can be— we're making life harder than it already is. Harder than it needs to be. Because God, no matter what you've heard, what you've read, or what you've thought about Him before, is not the one who's making this difficult.

God is all about keeping it simple.

We surrender, He satisfies. We trust Him, and He takes care of us. We love Him, and His love just comes spilling out of us.

The way to fullness is really not all that complicated.

Rainy Days and Mondays

Two of our students came to class soaking wet today. It's been raining like crazy lately, and a lot of the little tenement shacks down in Masi where they live are flooding out.

Masiphumelele (pronounced MAH-sih-poom-uh-LAY-lee)—"Masi" for short—is home to nearly forty-five thousand people, almost all blacks, many of them squashed together in families and groups of families in ten-by-ten shacks—or smaller—poverty on top of poverty. The whole area doesn't cover much more than two square miles, even with all those thousands of people in it, and the edge of town is only about a football field and a half away from us at Living Hope. I could throw a rock from where I work every day and hit ten shacks—and likely do some serious damage to them.

Unemployment there is enormously high. And probably 20 to 30 percent of the people are infected with HIV/AIDS, many of them suffering from TB as well. Add all of that misery together, and (as you'd expect) the rate of alcoholism is high, crime is high, domestic violence is high. It's rough. Rough place.

You haven't seen *poor* until you've seen Masi-poor.

So when these guys showed up in their wet clothes this morning, grimy and sticky—but still willing to come to work (would you? would I?)—I had a choice to make. An inconvenient one, and yet a simple one.

Actually, it made me think of the night a couple of years ago when I came home at dinnertime and noticed water oozing up through the grooves in our kitchen floor. After a little amateur investigation, I found the problem was originating from our laundry room, where a break in the pipes underneath the floorboards had dumped out gallons and gallons of water, and was still gushing.

Great.

My neighbor Mike had happened to pop in just as I was rocking the washing machine back and forth to move it, and he helped me patch up everything as best we could till I could arrange for a plumber to come the next day. But while I was griping and yammering to myself about all the trouble this mess was causing, an image came vividly to mind of Itai, who had come to work that very morning himself in damp, matted clothes, waterlogged from a batch of hard, overnight rains and a drenching walk up the hill to our campus. I remember how I felt, seeing him, realizing the daily obstacles that stood between him and his dreams for living out a new reality for himself and his family. And suddenly, my little home repair didn't seem quite so consequential or worthy of my complaining.

So when I prayed with my kids that night, asking the Lord to help us get our leak problem sorted out, I also made sure we thanked Him that we were warm and dry, not wet and cold. And we prayed hard for our friends in Masi, like Itai, and for their many thousands of next-door neighbors who brave the harsh elements every day, even when they're just sitting inside at home. We asked Him to show us how to serve them well and to use us as real sources of blessing in their lives.

That's just one small example of the simple heart change that comes from surrender. He makes us more aware of others' needs than we are of our own. He gives us real love for other people.

And you can't drum that up. Or at least you can't *keep* it up, not for long—not without deliberately choosing every day to fix your heart on loving Him, spending priority time in His Word and in His presence. When you give Him what He deserves and demands—when you truly give Him yourself—He simply gives you a mind that thinks the way He thinks, responds the way He responds, loves the way He loves. Instead of you trying so hard to generate it on your own steam and effort, He just does it through you. Automatic.

And nothing leads to more fulfilling opportunities than that.

So this morning, even though my first thought was to move on, to get going with our usual day, *God's* first thought was to love on these buddies of mine. And so once I got everyone else put to work, I rounded up a couple of pickaxes and shovels, and the three of us headed down into the township, where together we dug some trenches around their little shacks in hopes of redirecting the water, keeping it from pooling up in the middle of the floor again.

No, this isn't my job.

This doesn't grow cucumbers.

Doesn't help us make our bottom line.

And, no—you're right—it wasn't any big deal really.

But it *was* a simple choice to make—because loving God cannot help but result in loving people. It's just what happens.

Doesn't mean I do it right all the time. I'm still light-years away from where I want to be, in terms of being available and obedient to Him, always at rest and in agreement with following His lead. But I'm learning, as my pastor back home says, "You can't hold the ocean in a thimble." You can't love God the way we've been invited to do—the way we've been *commanded* to do, actually—without becoming a fiercely loving person yourself, so that even when you're just working or eating out or running errands or hanging with your friends and family, your primary thought in that moment is how to love the people you're with. To *be* love. To be *God's* love.

What a difference.

All I want to be anymore is somebody who is so wrecked and broken before Him, who is so in love with Him and so passionate about being more like Him, that everybody around me experiences His love, just by being there with me. And the reason I know this can happen is because I've found that the hard thing, actually—once you've given yourself over to loving God—is trying to be anything else *but* love to other people. You can't do it. You can't stuff it all in. It's like trying to hold your breath for five minutes. Something somewhere is going to explode—because when love for God is inside you, His love is coming out. You can count on it.

And, *man*, there's a lot of freedom in that. You don't have to go around any longer being concerned about how people are taking you, what they think of you, whether or not you're coming off as being sincere and genuine—because guess what: you just *are* sincere and genuine. You're projecting the love of God that's inside you without needing to spin it into something it's not, without dodging around the fact that you don't really mean it.

What a concept.

Trying to do the Christian thing without being in love with the One whose love makes the whole thing work in the first place—it's exhausting. We just end up turning it into a hypocritical waste of everybody's time, ours included. But nothing does what loving God can do, because it aligns us more and more naturally with the way He's created us to operate. And it puts us in the best, most blessed position to love others as an automatic by-product of our relationship with Him. You don't *try* to love; you *are* love. He fills you, and you fill others. With love.

It's that simple.

Just Breathe

When I stop to process what God has shown me in these past few incredible years, that's what surprises me the most: just how simple most of it is—and how it simplifies our lives as a result. Isn't that what we're all wanting? Simpler lives? It's what God wants for us too. Makes me wonder why we fight Him so hard on it most of the time.

I remember, for example, coming across that passage in Acts 17 where Paul was addressing the philosophical crowd in the Greek city of Athens. He had been stuck there waiting for his friends Silas and Timothy to arrive and catch up with him from their previous stop. You and me, we probably would've just holed up in our hotel room until they got there, chowing down on the free breakfast waffles and watching *SportsCenter*—especially if, like Paul, we'd basically been running for our life in every town we'd passed through on the way there. Seems like it would've been a good idea to lay low for a while.

But Paul? No, "his spirit," the Bible says, "was troubled within him when he saw that the city was full of idols" (v. 16). So he hightailed it over to the synagogue, walked up to folks in the marketplace, basically went all over town trying to set people's minds straight with the power of the gospel and the logic of his arguments.

What drove this guy like that? How could he be so bold, so fearless, so single-minded? What made him so passionate about his mission, so free in how he lived out his calling, always seeming to flow so naturally inside the will of God—the way all the rest of us wish we could?

It was really pretty simple.

The people who lived in Athens, just to be sure they didn't tick off one of their countless gods and goddesses by failing to worship them properly, just to be sure they hadn't overlooked any potential channel of divine blessing that might be available to them, had built a spare altar that was generically inscribed "To An Unknown God." Covering their bases.

Oh, that's perfect, Paul thought, when he saw it. And when his chance came to speak to the citizens at large later on, he decided he'd just introduce them to this "unknown" God, the One they'd left off their list because they didn't know His name, the One who "made the world and everything in it," who doesn't live "in shrines made by hands . . . as though He needed anything" from us, and yet who because of His great love for His creation "is not far from each one of us."

"In Him we live and move and exist," Paul said (v. 28, emphasis mine).

That statement just sears right through me. In fact, I love it so much, I've plastered it at the top of our website in big, bold, block letters. It even hangs on one of the walls in our bedroom. I repeat it to myself probably every day, often at multiple hours of the day. I don't want it to ever stop reminding me that there's only one, simple reason why I'm here: *because of Him.* And because of *that*, I'm free (like Paul was free) to follow this passion He's placed inside me wherever He wants to take me.

So I don't need to spend a lot of time worrying about whether this South African adventure of ours is going to kill me or not, or whether He'll keep my family safe, or whether I've made the biggest mistake of my life by walking away from a well-paying job to come here.

Because in Him, I live.

I don't need to get all hung up, thinking God's will is like some kind of treasure map to decode, afraid I might miss it by a couple of feet if I misinterpret a certain feeling or prayer or Bible verse. No, I can just release myself into experiencing a vibrant, surrendered, You-decide relationship with Him, knowing He'll never lead me astray. I'm free just to follow.

Because in Him, I move.

I don't need to be concerned that I'm spending my life on the wrong things, or that I'm missing out on something else by being here, or that people aren't paying me enough attention, or that I'm not getting recognized and given the proper amount of credit, or that my needs are going unnoticed and may not be met if I don't raise a big stink about it.

Because in Him, I exist.

Everything I do, everywhere I go, every move I make is under His complete control. I am being held together right this minute by the most powerful force in the universe. Is that not good enough for me? Think of the confidence and boldness I should feel because of that.

And the same goes for you.

So why the long face? Why the fear and lack of freedom to trust Him? Why the strain and difficulty with just being yourself, being authentic, being who He made you to be? Why the double-mindedness and confusion about whether to sell yourself out in service to Him, to be fully obedient to your calling? Why this knock-down/drag-out battle of wills, resisting what He's showing you, thinking your way is safer, more secure, more sensible than His?

And why the hunger for seeking substitutes—modern-day idols—that only "live and move and exist" because of *you*, because of how much and how often you're feeding them (whether it's money, career, education, exercise, sports talk, crime dramas, NASCAR, collectibles, whatever), when the one true God is inviting you into the full experience of just living and moving and existing every single day with *Him*, stepping out of the house each morning to the danceable rhythm of His will.

You sure you've got something better going for you than that?

I've never been the same since I realized, based on the truth of God's Word, that everything I need in life flows through Him. I live and move and exist in Him. *I'm completely covered.* Not because of anything I've done or can do, not because I'm any more special than anybody else, but merely because He is God and He's made me His child. He has put me in a place—not in South Africa, but simply in surrender—where I am free to explore with Him the far reaches of what He can do through me.

And that just simplifies a whole lot of things.

Burning Questions

Some of His simple truths, however, are much harder to take than others. They're still freeing. I'm not saying they're not. They help us fill out our days with meaningful ministry to others, to our spouse, to our families. And yet they're hardly United Nations speeches. They deal realistically with the fact that we live in a messed-up, busted-up, fallen-down world. You can always count on God to shoot straight with you. To tell it like it is.

And, boy, did He ever take me to school on one of these realities, not long after we got here—the Monday morning in late autumn when we heard that a fire had broken out in Masi overnight. More than sixteen hundred shacks had burned to the ground, leaving about six thousand people displaced, all their belongings destroyed.

It was . . .

Oh, pick a word. *Terrible.*

By the time we were able to get down there to see if any of our friends had been directly affected, it just looked like a giant scrap heap. Tin walls and roofing panels were scorched and twisted and lying everywhere. The stench of stale smoke hung in the air. People were sitting despondently on piles of debris that used to be their homes—homes that were hardly more than piles of debris to begin with—and yet it was all they owned. It was all they had. And now it was gone forever, with absolutely nothing to replace it with.

I'd seen a lot of heartbreaking things in those first few months since we'd arrived in Africa. But I'd never seen anything like this. And I'd never felt more hopeless, useless.

I remember just walking around with Bristol on my shoulders, hearing the cries of anguished mothers, seeing burned-out squatters trying to take some sort of responsive action to the tragedy that had struck them, to the losses they'd endured. It was pitiful, pathetic. To make matters worse, thick storm clouds loomed in the distance, sure to make a soggy mess of anything that hadn't already been ruined beyond all use. I was at a sheer loss for what to do. And yet in my natural, American, humanitarian bravado, I approached a man whose home was now little more than a mound of smoldering soot, and said to him, in a compassionate but rather upbeat, hopeful voice: "What can I do to help you? Where can I start?"

You can start, dude, by cashing this reality check.

I'm sure I'll never completely know what that look on his face was intended to mean. I'm aware I can never fully grasp what it's like to have *nothing*—to stand there guarding your little postage-stamp, square plot of land, trying to prevent anyone else from laying claim to it and building on it, seeing your little kid sitting emotionless on the ground at your feet, surrounded by the charred flakes and ashes of your only possessions, without a red cent in your pocket or a Home Depot anywhere in sight.

"*Help* me?" he said, sort of sarcastically—and definitely rhetorically. Total loss in his eyes, total despair and defeat. "What can *you* do," he said, "to help me?"

And I didn't really have an answer for him.

You got one?

He wasn't being rude. Just being honest. Seriously, what kind of magic potion was I going to pull out from behind my back that could produce anything of real value to him, to a guy whose material life was in utter shambles, burned to a crisp? By that night, I'd be back up in my house, all my kids tucked in bed asleep, hearing the rain slanting sideways against the window panes, feeling just a tinge of the forty-degree chill outside, the same wet cold that was shivering through that man's bones a mile away, with no roof over his head and no rebuilding plans covered under his insurance policy. He knew it. I knew it. And he was the only one of us realistic enough to say it.

"*Help* me?"

Yeah, right.

I'd like to see what you can do to help me.

We did do what we could. We manned a food collection point where people could drop off items to be distributed to the families who'd lost their homes. We picked probably a thousand cucumbers, I'd say, out of our own tunnels to put in the bins. And more than anything, I guess, we just went down there . . . to be with them, to hurt with them, to grieve with them, to hold them, to love them.

People can say, "Y'all should've just opened up your homes, let them stay as long as they needed, buy them clothes and basic necessities, raise the money." But, come on, you know as well as I do, we couldn't fix all the needs of all the people in that situation. I couldn't give enough, or hurt enough, or be broken up enough, or work hard enough to put even that *one man's* family back together, much less six thousand others. It was too big. *TOO. BIG.* Way bigger than I was.

And I'll tell you, I struggled with my feelings about it for a long time as a young, new missionary—the discouragement that knifes through you when you see so much brokenness and loss, when you see such a lifelong history of lack and despair, suffered by so many people over such a wide area. Why even try, it feels like, if this is all that's left at the end of the day, after you've done everything you can think of to do, sacrificing as much as you can possibly afford? There's not enough money in all the world to fix all the problems around here. Not enough food. Not enough medicine. Not enough raw materials. Not enough time. I don't care what kind of messiah complex pumps me up into thinking I can be everything for them, do everything for them, save the world, be the hero . . .

All I can do is live, and move, and exist.

Every day.

In Him.

And everything else, well . . . that's God's job to take care of in His way, using all kinds of people and all kinds of circumstances that are all at His kingdom disposal.

This doesn't mean, of course, that you and I can just casually turn away from people, ignore them, convince ourselves they're not really in as much need as they appear to be. But it does mean we're only here on earth to *serve* Him, not to *substitute* for Him. We'll flame out and be of no use to Him at all if we consistently feel the pressure to try doing His job all by ourselves.

Sure, there are things I can do. There are things He's put in my bucket. I can care for the people who are right here in front of me. I can hire a small fraction of them to work in our tunnels and be trained in our classes. I can make an extra trip or two down there to give someone a blanket, or a couple of chickens, or a pair of jeans my boys have outgrown. I can trust Him to show me the part I'm here to play, and I can let His love overflow through me in whatever ways He wants it to come out—at great sacrifice, with true generosity and selflessness, responding at the impulse of His guidance to real needs all around me. I'm tasked with carrying my part of the burden. And with doing it well. But God says that's enough for me to handle.

And I find a lot of release from that—my bucket, God's bucket. Courtney and I, sometimes we can get so worried about things, so fretful about how we're going to deal with something or manage the most recent challenge, whatever it is. And yet so often, we'll look at each other and just say, "That's in God's bucket, babe. That's for Him to figure out and show us what to do." And once we've flipped the switch to that mind-set, the simplicity that comes from trusting Him just sort of rolls over you.

You feel like you can make it.

Like you can do this. In Him.

So, no, not everything in life—not even in a missionary's life—is nice and clean, neat and tidy. Part of being surrendered, like it or not, means being put in situations where the volume of need is beyond what's humanly possible to counteract. But what I've found—what I'm finding—is that He'll help me decide what's in my bucket and what's in His bucket. And this keeps me freed up to give my complete attention to the people and opportunities He brings across my path. I'm able to totally live in the moment instead of feeling guilty, codependent, and distracted because of the twenty-five other things I could conceivably be doing. Instead, I can just be all here, be all His.

Live. Move. Exist.

Simply Speaking

The fulfilled life is a simple life.

Doesn't mean it's not very challenging. Doesn't mean it's not filled with a lot of unexpected surprises—both good and bad. Doesn't mean we won't meet up with some crazy experiences along the way.

But it's simple. It's built around simple things. It's built so that your decisions become less complicated to make over time because of decisions you've already locked down beforehand—like the decision to believe God's Word no matter what, like the decision to stay in constant prayer together as a couple, like the decision to think of others first before yourself, like the decision to work without needing personal recognition or affirmation or public credit for your ideas. It's a deliberate recalibration of your default settings—toward trust, toward faith, toward surrender—so that when faced with a dilemma or a confusing situation, no matter how hot the action or intense the battle, your initial inclination is to follow, to obey, to believe, not rebel.

It works.

I've *seen* it work.

And I've seen God do some powerful stuff as a result.

But the most important, most imperative ingredient in this simple, satisfying life is the same one Jesus prescribed hundreds of years ago, the same one given to the people of God many hundreds of years before that: "Love the Lord your God with all your heart, with all your soul, with all your mind, and with all your strength" and "Love your neighbor as yourself." Like Jesus said, "There is no other command greater than these" (Mark 12:30–31).

I'm more convinced than ever, from seeing it up close and in action, that 99 percent of our most effective work—whether in missions, in ministry, in our families, or just in the ordinary grind of everyday life—it all comes from love. When I get up beside these guys from Masi that we serve here at Living Way, when I spend time in the trenches with them, getting to meet them and work with them, they don't need me to be somebody who thinks he knows all the answers. They don't need somebody who's in love with how he sounds but not in love with the person he's talking to. The reason they open up to me and let me into their hearts the way they do is because of that one reason alone: *because I love them*. I really do. The renewed love God has given me for Himself has translated into a deep, sincere, and authentic love for others that I just never had before. And it's turned my everyday life into a truly satisfying life. Very simply.

I'd say I'm living, right now, just to live. Taking today for what it is, and tomorrow as it comes.

And I never want to live, move, or exist any other way.

Chapter 9

Living the Difference

T. I. A.

It's a little acronym we like to use over here—sort of like a rite of initiation, I guess. When people show up new to our ministry, maybe spending a few weeks short-term with us, or when family and friends pay us one of those special visits we love so much from folks back home, something will inevitably happen at an unexpected moment of the day, and one of us will pop out with a laugh and a shrug and a "T. I. A."

Can you figure out what it means?

I think I can probably show you better than I can tell you.

A while back, we were hosting a handful of people from our church who'd come over for a mission trip. Courtney and I had gone to meet them and to lead them back to the Living Hope campus. We were driving in our car, and they were following behind us in a van. Along the way, we passed a good-sized troop of baboons lounging off to the side of the road, as they often do. I knew this wasn't something our friends from Nashville were accustomed to seeing—these half-human varmints that roam the streets here on a regular basis and sit around like old men at the county courthouse. To people who are new in town, the sight of uncaged monkeys at close range is almost always worth a quick photo shoot and a story to tell their kids when they get home.

So I decided to ease over to the shoulder for a second to let everybody get some stills for their scrapbook. But while they were snapping pictures through the glass on the *right* side of the van, another baboon I hadn't seen at first began approaching from the other side, lumbering toward them at a decent clip. No sooner had I caught a peek of him in my rearview mirror, though, than he was up climbing, all fuzzy hands and feet, right into the tight space of a half-opened window.

He was *in* the van.

In their faces.

It was part *National Geographic*, part *America's Funniest Home Videos*.

My pal Rocky, former NFL linebacker, who was up riding in our car, was the first to dart to the rescue, hopping out and running at full tilt to sling open the sliding door and—I don't know, maybe think about putting a knot on that monkey's head or something. Thankfully, it never came to that (although it'd been a lot of fun to watch). Instead, I saw him give room as the intruder made his getaway, fortunately running off with no more than a handful of PowerBars—and not with my daughter Briley, who was also among the stunned passengers.

By this time, I had scampered back there to try helping out as well. But once it appeared the show was over, once the shrieks and screams had settled down into what sounded like relieved laughter, an apologetic smile crept across my face. And with hands extended in a "what're you gonna do" kind of expression, I could only come up with one thing to say.

"T. I. A., guys."

This Is Africa.

Yes, sir, this is where we Lankfords do life these days, and it can be pretty crazy, let me tell you. Still hard to believe sometimes that we're over here. Even after being in country for a few years, we're still trying to get used to certain things.

We'll be out to eat, for example, and right in the middle of our meal, a dog might come walking through the aisle, looking for handouts. We even went to one restaurant—a pretty nice place, actually—where a goat jumped over the fence outside and came tearing through the dining room. Before I knew what was happening, my son was out of his seat and chasing it out the back door.

T. I. A.

Most of the eating part, however, is really good here, just . . . different. Like, if somebody asks you over to their house for Saturday lunch, they'll expect you to show up at noon—which, of course, sounds normal—but don't expect to eat till probably around 2:30, 3:00. That's because it's not so much about the food as it is a time to hang out and fellowship, to relax together, to let the kids run around while the grown-ups feast on some uninterrupted laughter and good conversation.

But once the coals do get ready, the food is like a tailgater's paradise.

They call these little get-togethers of theirs a *braai* (rhymes with "try"). Same as saying a "cookout," because *braai* is their word for a barbecue grill. And from start to finish, a braai can go on for hours. It's just a big ol', nonstop meat fest, piled high with huge cuts of lamb and pork and beef and lots of other animal products you've probably never eaten before, almost always including some variation of *boerewors* (BOR-uh-vorz), which are sort of like a bratwurst on steroids. They're fat, juicy sausages, filled with who knows what kind of wild meat and seasonings, then wrapped up like a coiled snake and fire-grilled till you just want to—mmm!—man, they're awesome!

Let's just say, you wouldn't want to be standing between me and the serving line when they bring one of those things sizzling off the high heat. Because somebody's getting hurt. And it won't be me.

A neighborhood braai is about as South African as it gets. In fact, it's so much a part of the culture, there's even a movement that somebody's started where they're trying to set aside September 24 every year as National Braai

Day—a tribute to the backyard, South African spirit of community.

I think that's pretty cool.

And I wish you were here to enjoy one.

It's just another T. I. A.

One other surprising thing about life here is that just about every house in town enjoys the benefit of domestic help—a maid, a yard man and gardener, maybe even more. That's simply the rhythm of life in a part of the world that, even though it's definitely made some significant racial gains since the official abolishment of apartheid, still leaves many people depending on this kind of work in order to make a living.

Honestly, we weren't sure how to take it at first. Seemed a little uppity to us for a missionary family. We're here, remember, on the hardworking donations of our friends and supporters, and the last thing we want to do is not be good stewards of that. Like employing household servants, for example. But if we didn't participate, we'd be one of the very few folks around here who didn't. It's just how South Africa works, in context.

And that's how we got to know Cece. She had been "the help" for Jacques and Nellie (our first landlords) when they were still living here. She'd practically raised their son, Hayden. So when they decided to lease out the place, they naturally didn't want to leave Cece without employment and an income, having been so tight with her through the years. So we gladly accepted her as part of our lease agreement, and she's now become like a member of *our* family as well. She shows up here every morning, puts on her uniform, and does whatever needs doing.

I'll never forget, when that first house sold and we were needing to move out, she honestly didn't know what was going to become of her. So when I asked her, "Cece, you want to go with us to Capri?" she was like, "Oh, Mr. Joey, I didn't know if you were going to want me. I've been worried sick"—because the dynamic we enjoy with her is not indicative of a lot of homes and situations here. Some people can be pretty rough on their domestics. Belittling them. Barking at them. Making unfair, impatient demands. *Why didn't you iron my shirt? What's the matter with you?* But Courtney and the kids get along great with Cece. She loves us, and we love her. We were able, for instance, to pay for her grandmother's funeral expenses when she didn't know how she was going to manage it. So we're just tickled to have this kind of kitchen-table relationship with someone who blesses us so beautifully while we hopefully bless her.

And I'm probably spoiled forever to not clearing away my own dinner plates. Jealous?

T. I. A.

Africa is a different kind of place religiously. Ancestral worship and witchcraft are woven deep into the people's personal histories. One of the things I ask a lot of questions about is what some of these beliefs mean, and I've had a lot of interesting discussions with some of our students about where it all comes from and how it crosses the line once you understand the gospel and find your completeness in Christ.

It's a different kind of place economically, with the "first world" and the "third world" both existing within easy walking distance from each other. Bishopscourt, right outside where we live, is home to some of the wealthiest diamond traders in the world, mineral rights people who couldn't possibly spend all their money if that's the only thing they did from now till a week from next Wednesday. But then there's Masi, right there—the starkest kind of contrast imaginable. We live around it all. The richest and the poorest. At both extremes.

It's a different place relationally. It's different spatially. It's even different in just the normal speed of life. Everything shuts down around 8:00 at night. The shops close. People go inside. There's not much moving around after dark. Coming from the world of Waffle House, of course—being accustomed to twenty-four-hour grocery stores and all-night drive-thru—it was hard to imagine not being able to run out at 10:30 to get a gallon of milk or a milk shake if I wanted. But honestly, this one twist of lifestyle has turned out to be the most frustratingly brilliant thing that's ever happened to me. Being forced to cool my jets at sundown has been like stealing whole hunks of my life back. Incredible. I dare you to try it. You may feel like your granddad at first, but I promise you—you can learn to get over those late-night cravings. And once you've had a whole week of peaceful evenings at home and eight hours of sleep after that, you won't want to go back. Ever.

Being here is just very different.

T. I. A.

But my reason for taking you along on this little travelogue is not because I'm on retainer with the tourism department or getting a kickback from the chamber of commerce. I swear I'm not specifically trying to talk you into coming over here. I'm just using the analogy of South Africa and the differences Courtney and I experience on a daily basis to say that the *surrendered* life is a *different* life—wherever you go with it and whatever you do with it. If you want to know a feeling that's every bit as radical as living on another continent, just start choosing to "live and move and exist" in the confidence of God's plan and provision. And your life at the corner of Now and Normal simply won't feel like the same place as it did a week ago.

You'll spend your money differently, you'll go to church differently, you'll eat differently, you'll do your work differently, you'll treat your neighbors differently, you'll treat your spouse differently, you'll see your problems differently, you'll see your blessings differently, you'll hear the news differently, you'll look at yourself in the mirror differently, you'll parent differently, you'll think differently, you'll love differently, you'll act differently—you'll *live* differently. And unless I miss my guess, I'm betting this sounds to you like a *good* difference.

I believe you *want* your life to be different.

I don't know what feels the most rotten to you about where you are and what you're doing right now. Could be a recurring sin problem, could be a boredom factor, could be a strained relationship, could be an employment issue (or an unemployment issue), could be a bad case of stress overload and overcommitment—paddling like mad to keep the ship from keeling over while you're bailing water out at the same time.

Hey, that's not abundant life.

And that's not what we're meant to be stuck with.

That's what comes from doing the same old stuff, from living the same old way, loving the same things everybody else loves until you can't help but end up being like everybody else in the end. But you don't *have* to be the same anymore. You don't have to stay where you've been. Your life can be different. Better. Richer. Fuller. Surprisingly fulfilling.

I wouldn't say it if I didn't know it.

And so I hope this is what you've gotten from this book—that you can trust God implicitly to lead you to a different kind of life, one that's sure to satisfy your deepest desires for freedom, authenticity, and a meaningful future. And what I think you'll find—surprise, surprise— is that this life you're meant to experience is the life you'd enjoy the most if you only knew the way to get to it.

Well, God *does* know how to get you to it. So why not just follow Him there?

Gotta Love It

If there's anything Dave loves, it's being in his wood-working shop. Dust flying, saw blades singing, curls of new shavings piling up on the floor. He retired at fifty-five, was living in Washington State, and thought if he could somehow make a go as a freelance cabinetmaker, combining his skill and experience into a profitable business, that'd feel like the absolute best thing in the world to him.

What about you? What are the things you love the most? What are the gifts and passions God has placed inside of you, the things you could spend all day doing—the stuff you'd almost do for free if you were truly turned loose to focus on it?

Whatever it is, I can almost guarantee you, there's a need in the kingdom for it—which means there's a reason why God created you to be drawn toward it, to be good at it, to be able to lose a whole evening working on it . . . like Dave can, like what he can do with a hunk of lumber and a stretch of uninterrupted hours.

Dave's over here as a missionary now—making picture frames and furniture out of (get this!) scrap wood and shipping pallets. It's the most incredible stuff you've ever seen. A couple of his creations are in our house right now. True pieces of art and creativity.

But that's not all he's doing. When Dave first got here, he paired up with Lucas, a guy from Masi, to mentor him in the woodworking trade while simultaneously discipling him in Christian living. Starting with as little as

$2,000 or so in up-front investment costs (enough to buy band saws and such) they were soon leasing a spot in our building and cranking out 7,000 rand a month—upwards of $1,000—in frame and furniture sales. Just the two of them. High quality stuff. And whatever they earned after expenses went into a business account, set up for Lucas so he could eventually buy his own tools and equipment, fund a workable budget, and begin paying himself a salary. After a little more than a year, he was ready to open up a new shop under his own name, and begin training and discipling other young men going forward, the same way Dave had done with *him*.

So you tell me—Dave could be out in his garage back home in the Pacific Northwest, sanding down the detail work on another table or bookshelf or something, a custom job for a paying customer who wanted it just for a luxury . . . or he could be plugging into the life of a young guy like Lucas, showing him the ways of God while showing him how to turn warehouse litter into works of art.

Where do you think Dave is likely to find the most fulfillment?

And how much do you think he's loving the difference?

God doesn't want to waste your time turning you into a spiritual stereotype, forcing you to take on work that would be like your own worst nightmare, as if that's the requirement for being useful to Him.

The truth is, as long as there is human need, as long as there is brokenness, as long as there is poverty and hunger and generations of people who've lost all hope and direction, there will always be a place for your loves and passions somewhere in the world—even if that world is no more than a mile or two from your house.

Maybe that thing you love really *is* preaching or teaching. Perfect! But maybe you're not finding many opportunities to use it right now, at least not through the ways we usually think to go about it, like hoping to be asked to teach a Bible study or class at church or something.

Then quit trying to force it. Just surrender it up to God, put yourself in an obedient, available posture, and trust Him to guide you toward a place where that gift of yours can be turned into gospel-changed lives. (Including yours!) It may not end up looking the way you envision, but that's only because it'll look even better.

Your thing may be photography. May be writing or designing curriculum. May be a deep knowledge of gardening and composting. May be fishing or farming. May be animal husbandry or beekeeping. May be baking and hospitality. May be car restoration or ham radio operating. Just about anything you love and enjoy can be turned into a value-adding ministry—an inroad into another person's life—contributing toward the uplift and empowerment of somebody somewhere.

What a beautiful difference it makes when those things we're already passionate about are given back to God, infused with His wisdom, His timing, and His sovereign connections, and then transformed into sources of active blessing.

That's just the way He likes to do it. I mean, you wouldn't mind actually *enjoying* being on mission with Him, would you? Would that be okay with you?

Then get in. Get *all in*.

Because that's how abundant life works.

I can tell you, for example, after a couple of years over here, there are some things I really miss, now that we're living away from home. I miss snow and cold weather. I miss Thanksgiving Day and Thanksgiving dinner. I miss our friends and family. I miss the opening day of muzzle-loader season. When the first week of November rolls around, I just try not to think about it.

But at the same time, I've always loved being outside, outdoors, for as long as I can remember. And today my work is almost exclusively and blessedly indoor-proof. Spare me the ceiling tiles and cubicle dividers. Give me a blue sky and natural light.

I've always loved being with people, entertaining, laughing out loud and telling good stories (true ones, mostly). And because of where we live today, our home has never been so full of so many different kinds of people, on so many days and nights of the week, with so many opportunities for my kids and us to enjoy incredible community.

I've always loved hunting and fishing. I really hated the thought of giving that up, if I had to. And yet today, I've just traded our back-home area lakes for the Atlantic Ocean, and I've traded turkeys and whitetail deer for impalas and antelopes and the kind of big-game stalking that'll grow goose bumps on your goose bumps. Next time you come for a visit, how 'bout we take in some of that. Want to?

All I'm saying is this: I promise that what makes me happy here, happier than I've ever been before in my whole life, is one invaluable thing—the experience of serving God exactly where I know He wants me to be. As long as I know that, my destination could be anywhere. Whatever I needed my life to be before, all those years when I was doing everything else, this is all it ever needs to be from here on out.

But, hey, look what else He's given me in addition. Look how well He knew the desires He'd fashioned in my heart, even as a young fellow. Look at the lengths He's been willing to go for a country boy like me, giving my personal fulfillment the full-service treatment.

I'd say from the look of things, there's just a whole lot to like about the surrendered life.

Full Circle

I could tell from the funny smiles on their faces when I came walking into the tunnels one mid-afternoon, the guys were trying to cover up something they'd done, or were maybe not wanting me to hear whatever they'd been talking about.

Yep, there was a secret, all right.

But it was a good one.

Itai was back.

I told you earlier how, at one point, after some of our discipleship conversations, Itai had come under a personal conviction that he needed to go home and clean up a few matters concerning his travel documents. Several weeks had gone by since he left, until one day I received a collect call from him, asking if I could wire 300 rand for a train ticket back to Cape Town. *Of course.* But that simple transaction was followed by ten more days. And still no Itai. I tried not to say much about it, tried not to get everybody panicky, but I was getting worried that something terrible might've happened to him. It wouldn't have been the first time we'd heard stories like that.

Turns out, I wasn't far off.

He had been arrested at the border, even with all his paperwork revised, and was told they were sending him back to Zimbabwe, that he wasn't allowed through, couldn't return to his family. Big trouble. The truck, they said, was on its way and would be there by morning to cart him off. So he sat in jail all that night, crammed with a bunch of other people into a large, single holding cell, stripped of his phone and money and camera—everything except for his Bible. All he knew to do was to sit there and read. And pray.

Before long, two or three other men, who identified themselves as believers, had worked their way up close to him. And together they spent several hours in ongoing prayer—increasingly *loud* prayer—until they were actually erupting into praise songs, like Paul and Silas in the book of Acts . . . only in a different century and skin color.

The other prisoners yelled for them to be quiet.

They sang all the louder.

When morning came, the guards shuffled by to tell them the truck had broken down, that another one was being sent in its place, and that it would be there the next day. *Shut up and go to sleep.* But they just kept praying. People would come over to them and ask what they were doing, why they were praying like that, why wouldn't they stop. But Itai and his friends would just them tell about Jesus, tell them about the disabled truck, tell them about what a God can do when He's actually alive and can hear His people calling to Him.

The next morning brought word that a *second* truck had broken down, that they'd just need to sit tight, that a truck would get there eventually to yank them back to Zimbabwe where they belonged. But the border police obviously didn't realize Who and what they were up against. They thought they could be as ornery and arbitrary as they wanted to be and impose their judicial will on these men and this situation.

Guess what. No truck ever came.

Itai was released.

And I wasn't sure, hearing him tell the story to the whole group of us there at work, whether to cry or shout. I was half relieved, half excited, and 100 percent, totally inspired. Epic story—with the main character right there in front of me—all 120, soft-spoken pounds of him. I don't think I'd ever stood that close to true persecution. And true faith.

"But I didn't mind being in jail," he told us, not even acting like he'd done anything all that spectacular or unusual, "because I knew I was where God wanted me to be, and I knew I was doing what He wanted me to do."

And me, I knew at that moment, I was in the right place too.

Courtney and I came to South Africa to be a blessing to the people here. But every time I pull into the driveway at our house, and every time the plane touches down on one of our return trips to America, believe me, I get the message: I'm the one who's most blessed. I'm the one who's being filled up.

I suppose it's normal, coming from a position of resources and abundance, entering situations where people are benefiting from our experience, generosity, and expertise, to feel like we're doing all the contributing here. We give; they absorb. We're the rescuer; they're the rescued. But one of the most beautiful, soul-sanctifying things God ever does for us is to bless our lives through the ones we've come to bless, to expose the pride and superiority that makes us think we're in perceived control of them, and to realize that God is the one who's truly in control of all of us. Sure, people learn and grow from what we do, but we learn and grow as well by being in their company.

It's been a fine place in my journey, realizing this.

I think of what it took to get us here—efforts and decisions that seemed so herculean to us, massive, gut-wrenching levels of separation and turnover. Such a huge undertaking. And yet when I feel myself floating back into the ocean of what God is doing all the time, all over the world, in places like this and with people like these . . . and He's letting us be a part of it? People with *my* kinds of flaws and weaknesses?

We are eyewitnesses this very afternoon to moments we would never have been able to see and feel from our couch in College Grove. We've got front-row seats to spectacles of God's power we would've missed if we'd stayed behind.

I'm not *glad* God brought me here. I'm *blown away* that God brought me here. I'm humbled beyond belief that He's drawn me so powerfully into surrender, that He's done for us what He'll do with *anybody* who finally just gives up and says, "Here, God—You do it. You take it. You take over. I can't do it anymore."

This whole thing started out with me saying and thinking, over and over again, "There's got to be more to life than this." And the answer is yes. Yes, there is.

I just never dreamed how much more there really was.

Why Wait?

I preached my first sermon at two years old.

The only people in attendance were my little infant brother, propped up on the sofa, and my mom, playing the piano. My pulpit was a dining room chair, turned sideways, and my delivery was, I'm sure, nothing more than a high-pitched stream of consciousness. But if her memory holds, my mother tells me I gave them the full, capacity load—the Bible thumping, the invitation hymn, dropping down to one knee, praying for the people in my invisible congregation to come to the altar.

Apparently it was quite a show. My mom tells me that I gave more than a few encore presentations at family gatherings, including one at my grandmother's house, the day she and my parents were entertaining a visiting pastor for Sunday lunch. After I'd stirred up the heavens with my preaching and praying, Mom recalls this minister turning and saying to everyone, with a voice of prophetic authority, "The Lord has His hand on this young man. You just wait—God is going to use him in a mighty way."

I think all I must've heard was the "you just wait" part.

Because twenty years of rowdy shenanigans later, we were all still waiting. And after ten more years of settled-down complacency, I may have cleaned up the act a little bit, but I was still a "long way" from living in a "mighty way." Thirty, forty, fifty years more, and I could've turned my nice, little life into a nice, little lifetime. In fact, that's exactly what I had in mind.

But there's one thing I hadn't counted on. The one thing that changes everything.

The Lord had His hand on me. On us.

Just like He has His hand on you.

And what we can't do, won't do, don't know how to do, probably don't want to do, seeing what all we've got going at the moment and how much it's likely to cost us . . . *He* can do. He can change our hearts, change our goals, change our minds.

Change our lives.

Transform us. Fulfill us.

And that's what I'm praying for you.

You could wait, of course, but you don't know what you're missing. You could decide this whole thing sounds too radical to attempt, but you're the one who'll have to live with that decision in the end.

Or you could just surrender. Into those hands.

I promise they've got you.

Acknowledgments

I want to start by saying thanks to my wife, Courtney, and our five kids: Briley, Braxton, Barron, Bristol, and Baylor. You guys have been unwavering in your support of what God has called our family to do for His kingdom. I have enjoyed a front-row seat in watching as God works through you to bring hope and love to His world. You each have contributed many "stones to my stack."

I want to thank my parents for always loving me and encouraging me to reach for God's greater plan for my life. You provided the foundation for the work God has called me to engage in. You remain my example for love, faith, patience, perseverance, and a godly marriage.

I want to thank my in-laws for providing my wife a home that pointed her toward Jesus Christ. The disciplines that I admire in her were formed through years of consistent love, prayer, and guidance. I will forever be indebted to you for allowing me to walk life's journey with your beautiful daughter.

To my home church, your love and support have blown us away. We know there have been a lot of logistical things on your end that have supported us—things we will never know about. We are grateful to you for "running us off" and then "holding us up" while we engage in what God had called us to do.

To the West Sunday school class, you guys have continually inspired us to press deeper into Christ and His kingdom. As we watch from the continent of Africa, we see you doing things that are "lighting up" those spaces and places around you. You have given and prayed consistently for us since the beginning. And for that, we are eternally grateful.

To my dear friends Allen West, Sonny Terrill, and Rocky Calmus, you guys mean more to me than you will ever know. Your encouragement, love, support, prayers—and a kick in the rear at times—have given me confidence and strength when I needed it most. I love you, your wives, and your families dearly, and I thank God for allowing me to journey with you.

I'd like to say thank you to John and Avril Thomas, and Living Hope, for taking us in and teaching us how to be the hands and feet of Jesus. Thank you for creating the space for our skill sets and for allowing us to flesh them out within your great organization. Thanks also for modeling perseverance for us when the road gets a bit bumpy. Kingdom work is difficult, and I am deeply grateful for all you have done and continue to do.

To Richard Lundie, Melissa Shaw, Jennifer Pins, Matt Pringle, Taylor Nash, Chris Benton, and Scott Drennan—it has been an absolute pleasure to work with you. Your pursuit of Christ and His kingdom has blessed me beyond words. When I look at the people that God has brought to this endeavor, I can't help but get excited by the great things He's going to do through it! You have been a great team to serve with.

To my African brothers and sisters (too many to name), my life is better because of you. I am truly the one most blessed by this entire journey, and I will forever be indebted for the impact you have made on my life. I love you all and I thank you for allowing me to serve on your wonderful continent.

To the B&H crew—Lawrence Kimbrough, you are one of the humblest and most patient men I've ever met. I am so thankful to have been given the opportunity to write this book with you. I consider you a dear friend and brother. Devin and Dave, without your guidance, patience, and belief in this book, it would've never gotten anywhere. Jed Coppenger, thanks for being a true, life-long friend. I love you and your family dearly. Y'all truly are kingdom dudes, and I am honored to have worked with you! Thanks for everything!